C000174498

'T WAS A PROPER JOB

John Greenslade

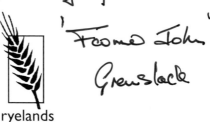

I hope you enjoy the book

'From John'
Greenslade

ryelands

First published in Great Britain by Ryelands, 2010

Copyright © 2010 John Greenslade

All rights reserved. No part of this publication may be reproduced, stored in a retrieval system, or transmitted in any form or by any means without the prior permission of the copyright holder.

British Library Cataloguing-in-Publication Data
A CIP record for this title is available from the British Library

ISBN 978 1 906551 25 4

RYELANDS
Halsgrove House,
Ryelands Industrial Estate,
Bagley Road, Wellington, Somerset TA21 9PZ
Tel: 01823 653777   Fax: 01823 216796
email: sales@halsgrove.com

Part of the Halsgrove group of companies
Information on all Halsgrove titles is available at: www.halsgrove.com

Printed and bound by Short Run Press, Exeter

FOREWORD

"Farmer John" decided to write this book, so that future generations would be able to have a record of his research into the
history of the Greenslade family and Way Farm in the Exe
Valley. Too many times I had passed the comment "I wished I had asked
father" but had left it too late after my parents were no longer around. I feel
fortunate that, after having born on the farm, all my farming experiences
and the changes made in seventy years, were passed on to me by my
parents. During the war, and after, times were "hard" and their long work
hours in keeping the farm together has been rewarded in me being able to
continue building an area of outstanding natural beauty.

The support of my parents and family has allowed me to give time to
the Young Farmers Movement from which I have reaped much reward.
The training at the Young Farmers Club helped me, and has given me the
confidence in becoming a Magistrate, a Radio Devon contributor, a trustee
of charitable organisations and to promote the retention of many countryside traditions. Our conservation work on the farm is, hopefully, there for
many to enjoy in years to come.

Thanks must go to my sister Margaret for her long research into the family history and her poetic contributions which I am sure you will enjoy.

As a non-computer literate farmer, I spent many a wet day using the kitchen table as my office where I am sure my wife, Jan can reclaim the kitchen as her domain. I would wish to thank everyone who has been part of my life's journey, however big or small. Without those of you who have jogged memories of times passed, and your support I might not have achieved my goal of completing this book. Special thanks to my grandson, Alex who patiently typed this book to present to the publishers, for my handwriting is not that legible.

Thanks to Mike Richardson for his help with the photographs.

I hope you will find that to date, I have led a varied and interesting life with memories I have recorded for your interest.

Proper job!

CONTENTS

PART ONE
THE FARMER

Chapter One	Who Do I Think I Am	9
Chapter Two	Way Farm and My Introduction	17
Chapter Three	Earliest Memories	23
Chapter Four	Changes in Farming Life	41
Chapter Five	Changes to the Farm 1988 -	49
Chapter Six	The Young Farmer's Experience	61

PART TWO
THE OTHER SIDE OF LIFE

Chapter Seven	Twenty Years Experience of a Magistrate	71
Chapter Eight	Farmer John on Radio Devon	79
Chapter Nine	Mid Devon Show, Shearing, Ploughing Matches and the Silvanus Trust	85
Chapter Ten	Trees, Ponds, Wildflowers and Wildlife	95
Chapter Eleven	Bits and Pieces of Fun and Life	103
Chapter Twelve	'T Was a Proper Job	112

PART ONE

THE FARMER

Farmer John aged three.

Opposite: *Two of John's family in Canada.*

CHAPTER ONE

WHO DO I THINK I AM?

My father was William John Greenslade, born in 1910 in Cadbury, the only child of John Tolley Greenslade and Mary Emma (Polly) née Tucker. Sadly Polly died when Dad was just 14 years old at Way Farm, Thorverton.

John Tolley Greenslade, born in 1876 was the first child of John Greenslade and Elizabeth (née Tolley), and was born at Cypress House, Witheridge. He was followed by three sisters – Hetta (1878), Evelyn (1881) and Margaret (1884). John was a shoemaker by trade in Witheridge and Cypress House is quite a large house, so their life must have been fairly comfortable then. But all this was to change dramatically when Elizabeth died in 1884 at the age of 34 years. The cause of death on her Death Certificate was given as pneumonia. She left John with four children aged from eight years to just a few months old.

The next we hear of Great Grandfather John was in 1886, when he re-married to Harriett Kingdon, a young lady half his age at just 20 years old. In the 1881 census it can be seen that Harriett was a servant of the Tolleys (John's first wife's parents), so we can only assume that she was probably sent to care for the four children after their mother's death. Surprisingly, Harriett had a son, Charles, two weeks after their marriage! Soon after this we know that John, Harriett and Charles left for a new life in Canada, leaving the other four children including our grandfather with the two sisters of their late mother. John apparently told them that he would send for them when they were all settled.

My great grandparents John and Elizabeth Greenslade.

John Tolley, Hetta, Margaret and Evelyn.

My great grandparent and his second wife who emigrated to Canada.

Great Grandfather John and two of his children in a picture taken in 1886 by a traveller.

Our Dad knew that his grandfather had emigrated, but did not know where or when. So some detective work was required. After Dad died in 1988, Mum gave us some photos, all un-named, and said that she understood that some were the children of John and Harriett in Canada.

There was a studio portrait of two young ladies with a clue in the corner – Alexandra Studios, Portage la Prairie, Manitoba. So using the computer we were able to pinpoint exactly the location of Portage la Prairie, find the name and address of the local newspaper and we wrote a letter enquiring if there were still Greenslades in the town. We were surprised to receive a letter from a young lady named Lori-Dee, née Greenslade. It all sounded very hopeful and she said her parents would be in contact when they returned from their holiday.

Meanwhile we employed a researcher specializing in Canada and she found for us a wealth of information. The 1901 Canadian Census showed John and Harriett with children Charles, William, Dorothy, Florence and Harry and also Harriett's mother and brother who appeared to have joined them in Canada in 1890.

The researcher was also successful in obtaining a copy of John's Homestead Report, showing every letter that John had written applying for land. Manitoba was advertised then as having excellent agricultural resources and important lakes and rivers – Lake Winnipeg is 260 miles in length – tremendous water powers, and great forest, fishery and mineral wealth.

The Homestead Regulations stated that every person who is the sole head of the family and every male over 18 years of age and a British subject, could apply for entry for a homestead consisting of one quarter section (about 160 acres). An entry fee of 10 dollars (about £2) was charged and the settler had to erect a habitable house as the homestead and reside in it for at least six months in each of three years. He should do some cultivation in each of the three years and at the end of that period he should have had at least 30 acres of the homestead broken of which 20 acres must be cropped. If the land was not suitable for grain growing, livestock could be substituted.

We wonder if this is what attracted John to go to Canada – the thought of owning 160 acres for just £2! Also Canada was the cheapest destination in the New World because of passages provided in the numerous ships that brought timber to England and had to find a return cargo. Also assisted passages were provided by Government grants and charities. So this option probably proved attractive to Great-Grandfather John and his new wife and baby son Charles.

But life must have proved unbelievably hard on the unbroken prairies and the winters were very hard and extremely cold. In the winters we believe that John and family moved into the town of Portage la Prairie where he made and sold shoes.

Harriett had nine more babies in Canada, three of which died as babies and also William (born 1890) died in his twenties due to diabetes. The Canadian researcher was successful in obtaining for us his obituary and death certificate, also the same for John himself who died in 1919 at Dufferin Avenue, Portage la Prairie.

We eventually made contact with Barry Greenslade (born 1938), son of Harry who was John and Harriett's seventh child born in 1899. Barry and his wife Ethel-Mae still live in the town; prior to retirement he had an insurance business there. They both came to England and spent time with us in Devon and Weymouth. From the first moment we hit it off and have become very firm friends. We have also both holidayed with them in Canada and met all the other Greenslades still in town. Barry and Ethel-Mae have three sons and two daughters, all with children of their own. So although our branch of Greenslades has no males to carry on the line in Devon, the family is still very much alive and thriving in Manitoba!

When we visited Canada, Barry showed us Greenslade memorials, the Greenslade homestead now farmed by Barry's cousin, Vaughan Greenslade, the house where John G. died in Dufferin Avenue, a museum showing a typical homestead in the late nineteenth century and the site of John's shop in Portage la Prairie's main street. We also met all his lovely children and grandchildren.

Opposite, far left:
*The Greenslade homestead
in Canada.*

Opposite, left: *Barry
and me in Greenslade Road,
Witheridge.*

Right: *Grandfather John
Tolley, my grandmother
Polly and my father.*

Below: *My lost second
family in Canada.*

When they visited us, we showed them Cypress House in Witheridge where our great-grandfather had lived with his first family. Barry and I had our photo taken beside the sign of Greenslade Road in Witheridge! We always have fun together and keep in touch by telephone, feeling we have found a long-lost brother and his family. It is unbelievable considering that a few years ago we didn't know each other existed!!

Going back to John's first family, we aren't aware if their father kept in regular contact with them, but we do know that he left each of them some money in his will, so hadn't completely forgotten them. But we believe that that they all had to work very hard for their aunts and uncles. We have heard in the family that John did send for them but they were proving so useful on the farms that they couldn't be spared.

Hetta married Fred Murch and lived latterly in Meshaw. Margaret married a Turl and the family were based in Aylesbeare, and Evelyn married a Webber.

Dad's mum was Mary Emma Tucker, known as Polly born in 1882 one of 7 children born to Edwin Tucker – born in 1853 – and Anna née Symons at Molland Farm, Chawleigh. Her youngest brother, the 7th child was Albert James and always known to us as Uncle Jim who was born in 1892. He was regarded as a phenomenon in Morchard Bishop where he lived and his reputation as a successful faith healer spread far and wide. Even the local GP used to refer people to him to have their warts and other skin complaints cured. When he was in his seventies mum and dad would take us to him for warts and ringworms and he could even manage to cure them on us, or animals just by a phone call!

My mother's side of the family had some interesting history. My grandfather was Maurice Paige Commyns Isaac and grandmother Kathleen Emilie (née Endacott), both born in 1892. Granfer Isaac – as we called him, was very strict and mum recalled how when all 9 were sat at the table, he only had to give them a look and that was enough! Mum also remembered that when the family lived at Bradford Farm, Uplowman, she and her older brother Jack walked daily down the road to Crazelowman, (about a mile) and then across fields to Chevithorne School – quite a hike and in all weathers!

When mum was just 11, she was sent to live with her Grandma Endacott after the death of their grandfather to help look after her and her bachelor brother Ralph Endacott. Mum cycled to Okehampton School. She cooked for them on an oil stove with a grate and open fire fuelled by peat. When she left school she went back for a while to help her mother with her six siblings. Mum told us about the tin bath in front of the fire and in the bath went the children one at a time from youngest to oldest! She remembered that the 4 boys slept in one room in beds and one night on checking them after they had gone to bed, the lamp had been too high and the boys faces were all covered in black specks!

In 1936, mum went back to Windwhistle, to again keep house for her grandmother and Uncle Ralph for 10 bob a week! Dad drove to see mum every Sunday and eventually mum and dad married in April 1939 and dad took over the farm at Way Farm from his father. My paternal great grandfather was John James Paige Isaac (1848 - 1923) and in the 1881 census he was with his family at Tounge End, Belstone in the heart of Dartmoor, Belstone being where we found his gravestone.

On the Endacott side of my mother's family our Nan Emily, born 1892, was the youngest child with older brothers – John, Harold, Ernest and Ralph (1883, 1884, 1887 and 1889 respectively). In the 1901 census they were farming at Gidleigh Mill with 2 elder sons working on the farm. In 1907, Harold emigrated to Canada and always kept in touch with his family at home, returning in 1924 with his wife and family for a family reunion as his father was ill and later died that year. In 1956 when our grandparents retired from farming they went on a three month trip to Canada to visit him and his family. Our Nan's diary of that trip is extremely interesting and descriptive. Including the ghastly, crossing from Liverpool which was the worst for many years.

The Endacotts for several generations before were mainly based around Throwleigh back to a Cornelius, born 1684.

Way Farm from the air and Way Farm map, 1930.

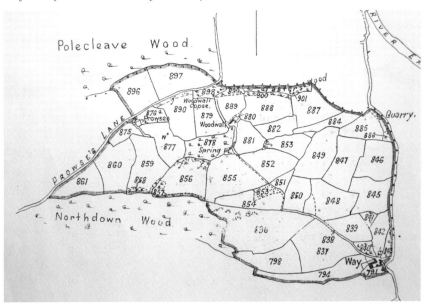

CHAPTER TWO
WAY FARM AND
MY INTRODUCTION

Way farm is situated in the Parish of Thorverton, Devon in the beautiful Exe Valley between Exmoor and Exeter. It has a red clay soil, with undulating land with not one level field on Way. Although in Thorverton Parish, most of the land overlooks the beautiful village of Bickleigh, and after more recent purchases land borders the River Exe whilst adjoining Bickleigh Castle. History shows that in Assize Rolls of 1306 it was called "Atteweye". In 1782 in the land tax assessments Way and Woodwalls were owned by Sir John Davey and farmed by Charles Paige and son Robert until 1805. Research in the Devon Record Office shows that at this time it was a farm of 82 acres, and called Way, Combhay and Spireaux. The map showed names of fields of which many remained in the 1939 tenancy agreement. At this time, Woodwalls was let as a separate farm, of thirty seven acres and contained five orchards. This included two fields above Prowses range called Hither and Yonder Down. The property which is now called Prowses was named "Bowden Hill". It seems that Sir John Davey was from Creedy, Crediton and had inherited these properties as a marriage settlement from Anne Lemon from Cornwall. The total acreage for the three properties plus North Down Wood was 172 acres. In 1832 it came into the ownership of G. S. Fursdon. Names of fields in those days were more important compared to today's DEFRA Ordnance Survey numbers. Interestingly fields now called Pondclose and Moor were called Higher and Lower Horse. Many other field names are similar as I know today, and should be retained in history. Many names are lost as farms are sold and split up.

The Fursdon family owned many other local farms as well as Way Farm. Grandfather (John Tolley Greenslade), took the tenancy of Higher Chapletown in Cadbury, this was a farm of 34 acres. Frank Butt and wife farmed Way from 1891, Frank died (after being bitten by a horse in 1912) but his wife farmed on alone until 1916. It was in this in year that John Tolley and Polly and my father aged six moved from Cadbury to Way Farm where he sublet Prowses as part of the agreement. Way and Woodwalls would have totalled 116 acres. Records from the Fursdon estate from this period of time were lost during the war when Exeter was bombed. My grandmother Polly died in 1924 aged 42 years of a cerebral haemorrhage. Whilst in Cullompton in the 1990s, I was fortunate to meet Manny Elston, who was in a nursing home there. He had wanted to meet me as he used to work for my grandparents at Way. He vividly described the day Polly died. They had slaughtered a pig that day, and gran always went to bed at 9pm, whilst granddad would go up at 10. He found her in a serious condition and asked Manny to get a horse from Way Mead and ride to Tiverton to get a doctor. He told me that it was raining "Cats and Dogs", and the horse was difficult to catch. Eventually off he went, and at Bickleigh Castle, the river was now in flood in the road. At Tiverton he forgot to warn Doctor Pollock that the road was flooded at the Castle. When he got back there the doctors car was stuck in the water, and by the time he had reached the farm, Polly had died. Manny said he was very fond of her. He also recounted how he used to take the horse and cart, to Woodwalls orchard and spend the day picking bramley apples, I still cannot understand how these apples did not get bruised knowing that the cart had no springs, and it was a rough journey home. If only I had met Manny earlier I would have learnt so much more about life at Way Farm. Sadly he passed away after my second visit to him. Interestingly I have found wages books for 1935 showing that Mr P. Conbeer earned one pound twelve shillings and six pence per week. Also at that time up to seven neighbouring farmers brought cows to the Devon bull charged at six shillings a time!

From grandfather and father's movement book, it shows that they took cattle, sheep and pigs to Bickleigh market up to 1949 and grandfather won a cup for Store Cattle in the 1930s. In 1939, my father after marriage to Marjorie Isaac of Butterleigh took on the tenancy at Lady Day at a rent of 160 pounds. At this time, grandfather had remarried and they moved to Manley Farm, Tiverton. They eventually retired to Worlington in 1953. In the tenancy agreement are many interesting parts, some of which are illustrated. Father's wages diary shows that Mr G. Howe was paid one pound fifteen shillings and six in 1939, which rose to one pound eighteen shillings, twelve months later. My history began on March 15 1940 when I was born in the farm house. By all accounts I was a fussy food baby, and mother was worried she would not rear me. But with help from my mother's sister Sylv and Mrs Way of Treymill, they got me through meal times. I have a letter from landlord, Mr G. Fursdon, congratulating them on my birth.

Previous history of land, researched by the Greenslade family.

Year	Source	Property	Owner	Occupiers
1306	Assize Rolls	"Atteweye"		
1782	Land Tax Assessments	Way, Woodwards.	Sir John Davey	Charles Page valued £4.19.0
1792	L.T.A.	Way, Woodwards.		Charles Page
1805	L.T.A.	Way, Woodwards.	Sir John Davey	Robert Page
1814	L.T.A.	No mention of Way or Woodwards		
1821	L.T.A.			
1832	L.T.A.	Way, Woodwards	G.S. Fursdon	Mrs Vinnicombe William Vinnicombe Mrs V's Brother-in-law
1841	Tithe Map	Way, Woodwards, Prowses, 154 acres in all.	Harriet Fursdon	William Wippell
1851	Census	Way		William Cornish wife and daughter
1861	No mention of Way or Woodwards, probably uninhabited at the time.			
1871	Census	Way Farmhouse		John Phillips (widower) with 8 teenage children
1878	White's Directory	Way		William Philips
1881	Census	Way		John Phillips (52 years) Farmer 200 acres 2 daughters, 3 sons
1891	Census	Way		Frank Butt Wife and daughter.
1893	Kelly's Directory	Way		George Butt
1916	Family Knowledge Prowses.	Way, Woodwards,	Fursdons	John Tolley Greenslade, wife and son aged six
1939	Family Knowledge	Way, Woodwards and Prowses.	Fursdons	William Greenslade and wife
1950	Family owned	Way, Woodwards and Prowses. Prowses sold off.	Farm bought by William Greenslade from Fursdon Estate for £5000.	
1975	Family owned	Way, Woodwalls and part of the castle estate.	Farmed to date by John W. Greenslade and Janette Greenslade	

Extracts from my father's tenancy agreement with George Fursdon of Cadbury which began on Lady Day 1939 for the rent of £160 paid on the quarter days of the year.

Covenants by the tenant include:-

1. To provide and keep a ladder or ladders in a fit state to use of sufficient length to reach to the roof of the highest building thereon.

2. To provide all reed for repairing roofs of the buildings and being allowed 40 shillings for every 100 sheaves, each sheave weighing 28 pounds and pay the thatcher's bill and find all spargads and cord which shall be required for that purpose.

3. To use the farm for agricultural purposes only and not permit any part of it for the display of advisements, camping or picnicking parties.

4. All hay, straw and chaff and green crops to be consumed on the premises.

5. To apply within 6 months after mowing not less than 10 tons of good rotten dung and not to mow more than once in any year.

6. To keep in order all watercourses and watermeadows and these to be stocked only with sheep from November 1st to April 1st.

7. To keep the gardens and orchards well stocked... properly trained, pruned and cherished and shall not permit any stock except sheep, calves under 12 months and pigs properly ringed to be pastured in the orchards.

8. To regularly kill rats and moles, cut all rushes and spud up all thistles, nettles and other weeds, as well as spread all molehills and anthills.

9. Not to use any part of the farm as a market garden.

10. Never to cut down, top or lop any timber, trees or saplings but to pay liquidated damages 20 pounds for every timber tree or

sapling which he or his workman shall cut down without the consent of the landlord.

11. To paint once in four years such of the external woodwork and ironwork of any dwelling house or buildings on the premises as shall have been previously painted.

12. On notice of leaving the farm the tenant with the last year's tillage for a spring crop to sow after the rate of 8 pounds of good clover seed and two pecks of artificial grass seeds per acre in all lands sown with spring corn on the premises.

Thereafter follows the schedule of fields and acres which totalled 151.922 of pasture, arable, orchards and coppice.

My grandfather John Tolley then gave an undertaking for the payment of the rent and the tenant's obligations.

What is extremely remarkable is that for more than 299 hundred years the names of fields at Way have remained mostly the same. Research at the Devon Record Office shows that in 1796, we had fields named in the tenancy agreement of 1939 such as Dry Close, Parsons Close, Pond Close, Five Journeys and Three Journeys. We found out that Five Journeys is named such because it is 5 acres, and it took a man and two horses, a day to plough one acre, hence Five Journeys took 5 days to plough and he would walk approximately 11 miles a day. We are not as fit today? In those days there was no need to run marathons or go to Pilates!! Let us hope that names of fields are not lost in the future as many have an interesting history.

In the hay field with my sister Margaret.

CHAPTER THREE
EARLIEST MEMORIES

I was born March 15th 1940, during the Second World War and probably not old enough to take note of the bombing, of Exeter at this time. We did make friends with the England family, who were builders in Exeter, who came and stayed at the farm during the worst of the bombing. I do remember that mother had blackouts on all the windows at night, which was enforced at this time. The perilous position that Great Britain was in during the war was not something I was old enough to realise. Farmers, though not called up for National Service, had to grow as much food as possible to feed the nation and the troops. Few imports were able to get here from the continent, and much of the work on the farm was done by horses, so there was rationing of food, up to and after the war ended. My sister Margaret was born in 1945, and shortly after father was diagnosed with Pemphigus – which is an uncommon serious skin disease, which in those days was usually fatal. But, Grandfather Isaac paid for a specialist from London to see him, and his treatment thankfully saved father's life. Whilst in hospital mother's brother Ralph stayed and worked on Way Farm until father was back on his feet.

Whilst my Dad was in hospital I wrote the following letter which has been kept to this day, at the time I was only six years old.

Dear Daddy
Thank you very much for your letter. I hope you are getting better and soon coming home with mummy, Margaret and me. I hope you will be home before Margaret's birthday. I am a good boy and help mummy feed the fowls and chicken and pick up the eggs. I have heaps of things to show you when you kum home. I think you will not know Margaret when you kum home. I have been catching rabbits. We caught 5 and they missed three, then I went in doors and got the gun and cartridges. Mummy rode the binder a little while before Jack Coombes came.

Lots of Love
XXX
From John and Margaret

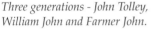

Three generations - John Tolley,
William John and Farmer John.

My sister and me riding bare back.

Memories of life in Way Farm House

There was no electricity or tap water at this time. Oil lamps and candles provided the light indoors, whilst the old Hurricane lantern (I wonder how it got this name) was the only light for any outdoor work until the Tilley oil light was produced. Water was pumped to the outside of the house by a water ram, which operates on the fall of water from a shallow well in Lower Spot. The hot water was heated in the wash house in an old copper boiler. In a channel underneath the boiler a fire was lit, for washing day and baths. Our bath was a tin (galvanised iron) one, and held between 10-15 gallons of water. This was placed in front of the open fire in the kitchen. To the right of the fire, was a black cooker, which was replaced in 1945 with a Rayburn solid fuel cooker. Wash day was usually on Monday, and was very hard work on the ladies with scrub boards and soda used for soap. Then she had to turn the old mangle by hand to ring out the water. The clothes line was the only drying facility while the ironing was done with a flat iron, which had to be constantly heated to the right temperature on the open fire. The large open fireplace had a huge oak beam, above the entrance, with hanging crocks for kettles, pots and pans. To the left of the fireplace was a bread oven, which I was told was last used by my great grandmother Greenslade, in the 1920s. On the right, was an entrance to a smoking chamber, where ham and bacon were smoked for keeping, and better tasting quality. I wonder why there was a need for this, for when the wind was in the wrong direction, the open fire smoked like blazes!

There was a large dairy at Way, which contained salters and shelves which held earthenware pots and bottles, for various ways of preserving food. Also on the floor were slabs of marble and slate which kept things cool. The dairy was on the north side of the house, where it was coolest and the shutter doors on the windows closed over a gauze covering to keep out flies. The salters contained saltpetre, in which pork was kept until needed. I well remember father regularly killing a pig or lamb, out at the back door (no health and safety issues then!). The hair had to be scrubbed off with boiling water, and the intestines cleaned out. The water came across the mead from North Down Wood, into the trough at the back door. Intestines were then used for sausage covers. One of my Saturday jobs was to make sure cattle did not block the water flow three-quarters of a mile away at North Down Wood.

In the dairy, mother kept cheese and she used a milk separator, which she used to make cream. Once the milk was separated, she would put it on the range cooker, in a pan. It was very important this did not boil, or else it spoilt the cream. On the marble slabs, she kept kilner jars and pots, which contained pickled eggs and onions etc. In wooden containers, she kept her flour from which she made cakes and bread. Potatoes were stored outside in the roothouse, whilst vegetables were cut and dug from the farm garden. Of course the flagons or firkins of cider were always on tap for family and the workers. The sanitary arrangements were rather basic, in those hard times. There were two outside loos which had running water underneath taking everything to the stream in Lower Spot. One was at the back door, fed from the North Down water whilst the other was next to the piggery and mealhouse some twenty yards from the front door – remember no soft toilet tissue in those days, just torn up newspapers, rather rough to the bum! The jerry pots under each bed, had to be emptied daily.

Kitchen furniture consisted of a large settle which cut the draught from the front door. In the centre of the kitchen was a large pine kitchen table, with forms either side of it. On the end was father's wooden-armed chair, which was the head of the table. The pine dresser held all the necessary plates, cups, knives and forks etc, which were all washed in an old white Belfast sink. The huge wireless stood in the window, and was powered by an accumulator – no dry batteries back then. The old sofa was not the most comfortable, as it was filled with old horse hair. Upstairs all beds were iron framed, with feather mattresses and pillows, usually filled with goose and hen feathers. Most bedrooms had a wash stand and mirror, and two of our bedrooms had fireplaces. I was born in one of these bedrooms.

Access to these bedrooms was from two totally different staircases, one being an oak spiral and the other being converted from the old smoking chamber. At the bottom and top of the spiral staircase, an axe had been used to chop away part of the uprights. Father told me that a Mr Butt, a previous tenant, had died upstairs, after being bitten by a horse, and they had difficulty bringing the coffin down the stairs. In later years, this was confirmed by relations of Mr Butt, who were now undertakers. It was explained that it had happened quite frequently in old properties at that time.

Food consisted of the normal meats, plus two regular pies, of lambs' tails and rooks in season. It was usual to cut off lambs' tails on Good Friday. There were no rubber rings used at this time, so a sharp knife was used by father to cut off the tails. The best were skinned, and put into boiling water, to clean and sterilise. Cooking followed when a pastry top was added. After May 10th young rooks would come off the nest onto the branches, and after being fed well by their parents were very well fleshed. They were easy targets to shoot, and their breasts were removed and cooked under a pastry cover. Pigeon Pie was a very similar dish. There were apple dumplings, with plenty of kitchen garden gooseberries, raspberries and blackberries, to eat for dessert. Drinks consisted mainly of tea (no teabags), Ovaltine, Camp coffee with plenty of cider.

Early transport was a Ford Eight car, not the most reliable but got us from A to B eventually. The nearest petrol pump was at the New Inn now the Trout Inn, Bickleigh – a 10 minute drive. Work outside the farm yard, consisted of milking shorthorn cows, on a three-legged milking stool and a tin bucket. Two saddleback sows had regular litters in the piggery, whilst two others were kept in the orchard, where our bungalow now stands. Father used to put copper rings in their noses, to stop them rooting out the apple trees. This was a noisy exercise, likewise when he castrated the young pigs. The stable housed 4 heavy horses: two which come to mind, "Madam" and "Short", I regularly took to the Thorverton blacksmith (Les Vowler) to be shod. I rode one with a West of England sack, as a saddle and led the other one on a five mile return trip. Wasn't my backside sore after an up and down journey! The roothouse stored the potatoes and mangolds with a talet above where all the spare reed was kept, for thatching. We used a root cutter, to shred the mangolds for the young stock. Either side of the root house was a cow shed, with stands for twelve cows, plus a yearling and calf house while hay and straw were stored in the loft above. The other main buildings in the yard were the threshing barn and the cellar that housed the cider barrels, whose contents were the most important for all the workers. The buildings were thatched when I remember them first. This was replaced with galvanised iron, by the Fursdon Estate worker, a Mr Lewis Gater: he completed this task all on his own, with just a ladder, working at quite a height – again no health and safety at that time! The barn was originally a threshing barn, the machinery driven by a series of pulleys from an attached roundhouse. In the barn, when I remember it first, there was a whimmer which blew all the douse and rubbish from the thrashed corn. There was a chaff cutter which was probably the oldest forerunner of the modern straw chopper. Fixed to the floor was a cake cracker, and roller mill, which combined created food for the cattle. In one part of the barn, was the wooden apple press, which was used annually. At the bottom of the cellar were the hogsheads of cider. At the top of the twenty-step stairs, was the corn store – we used to carry West of England sacks, which held two-and-a-quarter-hundred-weight of wheat, up these stairs. By the time you got to the top, your knees were beginning to buckle.

Below the barn, were a couple of sheds. One of them housed the most important animal on Way Farm. Father kept a Red Devon bull; as well "looking after" his own cows, up to seven neighbours brought cows to bull for several years. In was never a dull moment for him I am sure! In the early days, milk was taken from the cow shed, to the wash house, were it in went through a strainer, into solid 10 gallon steel churns. When full, they were hand rolled to the bottom of the lane, to a milk stand from which Bladen Dairies, Crediton, collected. Just behind the farmhouse was the wood yard, where all the fuel to keep the house warm and heat the water, was stored. There was always a faggot rick which contained starting material usually the tops of hedge cuttings. Against the hedge a huge amount of ash, oak and hedge timber stood in pyramid fashion; a wood horse was in the corner upon which we hand sawed all our logs. Under the slay at the back door, was a forty gallon drum of paraffin, used for our Tilley lights and oil lamps indoors. As time went by, our oil lamps were replaced with a Calor gas system, for downstairs. This system needed great care, that when lighting you did not break the mantle, whilst being lit by a match. In later years, this system was made redundant, when we bought an electric generator running on diesel. This system started when you switched on the first light, and stopped when the last one went out. Many a time, you went to bed, and frustratingly found out, that the generator had not stopped, because there was a light still left on. In the 1960s the main supply came to us from across the river valley, at Burn. The first postman, I remember used to walk all the way from Thorverton, but after several years, he was given a bike. The telephone first came in 1951 on a very similar route as the mains electric.

Labour on the Farm

My earliest memory of labour on Way was one of several different skills of the work force. One of my first memories was that of "Johnny the German",whose real name was Erich Hasse, who was a prisoner of war, and who lived in the house after the war was over. He was a super chap, who at first thought his family in East Germany were all lost in the bombing. But in the late 1940s at Christmas time, he learnt his wife was still alive and so naturally wanted to return. I remember seeing him in a full flood of tears, on hearing this news. After his return to Germany, he wrote every Christmas, and sent a doll to my sister Margaret as a present. We had several prisoners of war, who worked at the farm, coming from a camp in Tiverton, including Italians, who did not like hard work. A Mr V. Strong from the WARAG visited them, while they were picking up potatoes, behind Bickleigh Castle. They were not getting stuck in, so Mr Strong, said to them, "He would shoot Mussolini", and they downed baskets and walked all the way to the camp at Tiverton to never be seen again! Another prisoner of war, called Franz took a bottle to base one night, returning it next day with a model ship inside the bottle. We had a worker, called Basil Howe, who regularly earned one pound four shillings a week. Jim Maunder was our regular rabbit trapper, who also helped out at harvest time. He trapped rabbits regularly around the farm, armed with his spring traps – now illegal. Grouped in ties of ten, with his hammer and sieve, he worked in all winds and weathers. At Woodwalls he used to record his catches on the back of the wooden door for many years, and sleep overnight in the hay, so he was ready for an early morning round. Jim lodged with a Miss Crocker at Willis Farm, Bickleigh. I remember Jim telling us that when she went in to retire in an adjoining bungalow, that the bath had two taps! At threshing time, Jack Coombe and John Harris, both neighbours, came to assist with this work. Jack Vearncombe and his sister Grace also came regularly. Jack was my mentor for steeping and casting up hedges; Grace was an expert at picking poultry. Mrs Trump came out from Silverton on the bus, to help mother in the house in the early 1950s. It was at her house, I first saw television – the 1953 cup final.

1935 wage slip.

1943 wage account.

Transcription of letters from Johnny returning to East Germany 1950 (broken English)

Dear Family Greenslade
I should you communicate that I arrived home the 25th May at half night pm. After 14 days journey from the UK I came home the day I have long ardent waited. It is all in good putting order and health. It two few have altered, it is the old home.
I don't know my thoughts in the first moment . My wife has little two. They has lost thirty pounds and look fitter. They is without fat. On a personal note me think often of the nice butter, cream, mutton and meat which I could enjoy with you dear family Greenslade. Here is it is hard to live, for all that I am content after coming out of proson camp. How many people have lost their homes?
We have in the village 300 inhabitants and in time 300 fugitives. I have work in the village in a saw machinism. I work in the morning 7 o'clock, 1 o'clock dinner time and 5 o'clock finish, I can do my work at home which is many work for me. Now dear family Greenslade how are you?. How shall you be ready with many work. How are your my little darling Margaret and John?.
I will now make finished. Once more my best thanks for all your good things

what you do for me. Many greetings from my family with best wishes
Yours sincerely
Erich Hasse

Many regards to your parents and brothers and sisters.

Another letter received 1962

Dear Greenslade Family
I thank you very much for your letter of December 1961. I see you have not
forgotten myself. I intended many times to write to you but we have a lot of work
for every. I am glad you are well. We are healthy up to date and hope your
Margaret is a tall girl now. My grand daughter is eleven years old. My grandson
is three and I like him very much. It is a funny child!. We hope you had a merry
Christmas and a good beginning of the new year. We at television a lot of snow in
England. We always have a lot of poultry work. We had a goose and carp for
Christmas dinner.

In this year, we intend to buy a motor car I think we must have to wait some
months for it. We hope for fine weather as last summer was not favourable for our
agricultural. Last year in May and June it rained every day. The harvest in
potatoes has been very bad. We hope this year will be a peaceful one and we often
think about the last war time. Last summer we had a visitor in our village coming
from England. He visited his mother here. He had remained in England after
leaving the prisoner of War Camp. Now he has children and he is living in York.
Thank you for your invitation for us to visit but it is a dear journey for us. I think
your ministry in these days is not interested to see travellers from East Germany.
But with best wishes to you all, I remain as your Erich and family.

Livestock

Livestock at Way, consisted on the cattle side of mostly Devon or Shorthorn breeds. All these cattle had some very good "Antlers" (no dehorning
in those days), and after calving would easily unhinge wooden gates, to get
to their calves in the yard. Father kept about fifty Suffolk sheep and four
saddle back sows, which were crossed with a Large White boar. About one-
hundred Rhode Island Red hens were kept for egg production, and fifty
Indian Game chickens killed for the table on a regular basis. Several were
sold to the butchers, Hannafords and Lethbridges in Exeter who regularly
collected the eggs and chickens. We normally kept two sheep dogs, and a

terrier which was always on hand at threshing time for rat and mice control. Bickleigh had a livestock market in a field adjoining the Trout Inn car park. In early days cattle and sheep were walked to this frequent market. Father's movement book, showed that the market kept going under Dobbs, Stagg and Knowlman until 1949. We had a newspaper cutting, which showed that in 1935 at the spring auction, there were five-hundred cattle, five-hundred sheep and seventy-five pigs. My grandfather won a cup for store cattle, which were sold there. I also have memories of fetching feedstuffs from Bickleigh Mill with a horse and cart. The Bickleigh Mill was operated by the force of a huge water wheel, which ground the corn. It was run in those days by the Gay family. It was probably useful to the mill and the market that the railway station was so close, so that after livestock had been sold, it could be taken to other parts of the country. The station also brought in goods for the mill, as well as taking apples and sugar beet and probably passengers to where they were needed.

We were registered as a dairy farm in 1949 and became Tuberculosis free in 1955; our first vet was a Mr Mathews and then Griffith and James. It was necessary by law to dip your sheep annually and we used to walk them to Hawthorn Farm, where a policeman was always present, who also took samples of the dip.

In 1943 Father had a livestock valuation – shown below. His wages book showed that Mr T. G. Coles earnt £3 2s 6p a week. There is also mention of casual and Land Army workers.

Livestock	Each animal valued at
10 Cows	£33
3 Working horses	£45
1 Devon bull	£37
6 Calves	£6
16 Young stock	£25.10s
25 Ewes and lambs	£4.15s
1 Ram	£8
1 Sow	£5
2 Store pigs	£2
150 Fowls	9s.6p

Messrs Wood, Waller, Counter, Vearncombe, Vowler, Ellsworth and Walters brought a total of thirty eight cows, for service to the Devon bull at a cost of six shillings each. I remember in later years, that a neighbour used to let his sows out massing acorns in the autumn. They used to run from oak tree to oak tree, to feast on the recent fall of acorns. The problem was that they did not respect farm boundaries and as there was no electric fence, they made frequent holes in hedges.

Work in the Fields

Farm labourers, had strenuous and long periods of work. One of my earliest memories, was of dung heaps which were tipped in the fields twelve yards apart, and then hand-spread with a dung fork. Remember that prior to the heaps in the field it was loaded from the cattle houses into a dung heap in the yard, and then reloaded onto a butt cart prior to being taken to the fields – all this was done manually. All corn and root crops had to be hand hoed which included cabbages, turnips and mangolds – locally called wurzels. Mangolds were hand pulled in late October around Bampton Fair day. The tops were snapped off, and left to rot in the field. You were expected to pull three rows at a time, throwing them alternately to the right and left, so that the tractor and trailer could easily travel between the rows to make loading easier. They were then stacked in a "cave" against a sheltered hedge adjacent to the rick yard and covered with a little straw but then with "vearns" (ferns), which were cut from the top of Five Journeys to keep the frost and rain off. Cabbages were grown annually after the ground had been prepared: Flat Poll plants were purchased from local growers, and Messrs Chanin, Gleeson and Edworthy. These plants were tied up in bundles of 25, and cost one pound a thousand. They were dug at a yard apart in rows, which were subsequently horse hoed, to control the weed. When they matured, with a good solid "heart", we would cut them off, and load them into a trailer to feed cattle and sheep for the winter. The sides of hedges were pared with a staff hook, with the tops of the hedges left for 10 to 15 years, when the large wood was either axed off or cut off with a cross-cut saw. With the smaller varieties of hazel and willow steeped, then the sides of the hedges were cast up with a Devon shovel and a tubil (digger). The small tops were bundled into faggots, for fire lighting. Most of our meadows were watered by running water which was allowed to leak at various stages across the field. This was an annual job with the shovel – again done manually. Corn harvest

Hard work hay making.

First tractor – Standard Fordson on spadelogs with binder.

Heavy horse with mower with
my father and me.

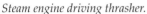
Steam engine driving thrasher.

was an extremely labour intensive job. Firstly the corn had to be weeded by hand, and if you failed to clear all the dashels (thistles), the handling of the sheaves could be a sharp experience. Before the corn was cut with a binder, the workers would cut around the fields with a scythe, and tie the sheaves up manually. We had an Albion binder which could be temperamental at times, especially the knotter. You would occasionally get small sheaves and some not tied that meant more manual retying. I remember loading a wagon full of sheaves with Jim Maunder and bringing it back to the rick yard across an uneven track. Jim told me to keep the horse and load in the tracks, but because the load looked unstable, I unwisely pulled out of the tracks only to see the whole load tip over. I was sworn at by Jim, for disobeying his order and as a punishment I had to reload the wagon by myself. Some of these sheaves had dashels in them, which made it a painful operation, but I noticed these sheaves made no difference to Jim's hands, for as a rabbit trapper he had hands of steel. Prior to collecting the sheaves from the field, they were stooked for a couple of weeks, for them to thoroughly dry out. The construction of the rick was an art in itself, for if not made properly, one would have to put wooden props, against it to hold it up. Any neighbours seeing this would ask who made the rick. The haymaking time was also hard work. Firstly the grass was cut with a finger mower; I have memories of my father sharpening the blades of the mower, and binder on the top of wooden gates (no steel gates in those days), held in place by a screw tight vice. It was imperative that the blades were sharp, otherwise you were stopping regularly to unchoke the bed of the mower which was not an easy task to undertake using horses as they would occasionally move. When blades were knocked out by stones or broken, we used to rivet in new ones, or take to the blacksmith to repair broken knives. The hay was then turned and raked with horses, and with a hay sweep taken to the rick side. Here with pitchforks it was then again painstakingly made into a safe hayrick. When it was taken for feed in the winter, it was cut out with a hay knife – a two foot narrowing blade. Occasionally when the hay was not made in perfect conditions, it would heat up and to prevent it catching fire, a four foot hole was cut through the middle, this being a very sweaty job, which needed many firkins of cider, to be consumed for refreshment. Work did not end here, as all these ricks had to be thatched to keep the winter weather off – no plastic sheets in those days. The reed to thatch the ricks was held on by hazel binds and spargads. Teatime in the harvest fields was an absolute experience when mother brought out the harvest tea kettle. An old white sheet was laid out with pasties, sandwiches and cake and the like – all work stopped for mother's tea, which is some different today as we eat as we work.

Machinery 1940-1949

Amongst our collection, were horse butt cart (tipper), hay wagon, corn drill, root drill, hay rake, hay turner, horse plough, spring time harrows, stone roller, Albion binder, drags and horse mower. The maintenance of the machinery was mostly carried out by blacksmith Les Vowler.

Ready for work!

Machinery 1950-1956

Our first tractor was a standard Fordson fitted with iron wheels and spadelogs, which was then later replaced in the middle 1950s with one with rubber tyres. It ran on petrol: to start it required a starting handle, and then turned over to TVO (tractor vaporizing oil). We then bought a Ransome self-lift plough, front-end hay sweep, and steel fold-over hay elevator. Several of the horse machines were converted to be pulled by tractor such as the binder, and mower. We had contractors who came here to do the threshing; they included Denners, from Cullompton and Sharlands from Thorverton. I remember a thresher coming pulled and worked by a steam engine, which upon reaching the farmhouse filled up with coal and water. A particular occasion at threshing, was rodent control – a small roll of wire netting was put around the outside of the rick through which the rats could not escape. The last 10 minutes was usually a sporting occasion, the terrier against the rat.

Holiday Memories

Memories of holidays stood out, especially when I visited Grandpa Isaac, at Worth Farm, Hele, were he kept a fruit farm. I always felt great sitting in the back of an old army lorry, which went around Silverton picking up the workers. He grew lots of apples, plums, strawberries and blackcurrants, and it was so easy to over indulge. One year, he bought my sister, Margaret an Exmoor pony from Bampton Fair, which was not fully broken in. Father asked me to ride it up to Prowses to ask neighbor Mr Coombe if he could come threshing next day. On the return journey it took off, throwing me to one side, as it jumped a hedge, and my love for horses has never been the same since. We always went to Worth Farm for Christmas Day, when after a superb lunch, we would all sit and sing around the piano while Gran played the music. I also spent holidays with Granfer Greenslade at

Opposite: *Characters at
Bickleigh market 1935.*

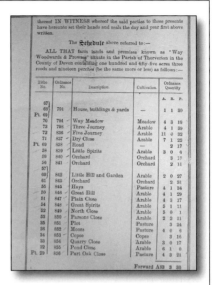

Clockwise from right:
*Schedule of farm fields;
My ID card during the war;
Blacksmith bill;
Trashing bill;
First rubber tyred tractor - note price.*

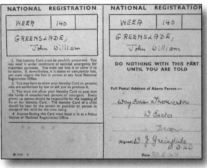

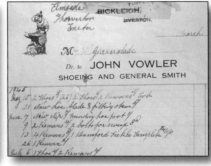

Worlington, and my memories were here of a beautiful chiming clock, which went off every quarter of an hour, and I found it extremely difficult to go to sleep! I also spent time in Bournemouth with Auntie Sylv where I experienced living in a town. At home we did not do much socializing other than visits to relatives, such as the Murch family at Meshaw, where I inevitably went to sleep, in front of the open fire before our journey back to Way Farm.

Buying the Farm

In 1952 father was offered the chance to buy Way and Prowses Farms from the Fursdon Estate for five-thousand pounds. To help finance this he sold about 200 mature trees to Yeoford Saw Mills, for timber use. Most were oak, which were sawn down, with a cross-cut saw and axe. At Woodwalls there were two large walnut trees, which were taken down and not

Way Farm house.

replaced until the year 2000 virtually in the same area. The firm told us they wanted the roots and stumps of the walnuts which were removed by digger and, although paid for, were still there some 20 years later. I have since planted ten walnut trees around the barn.

School Days

In my younger school days, I remember there were two old tramps (not gypsies), who used to camp in the words behind Bickleigh Castle cottages. Sometimes, we would creep up the old lane, which goes from behind the cottages through the wood to the Crediton main road, and spy on them as they sat around their smoky wood fire. Their sleeping quarters were under a couple of old green rick sheets, and I remember the two tramps would sometimes call at neighboring farms for some bread or milk. Although they looked fearsome, with their long white beards, they were actually very polite and harmless. This site was their home for several years.

To earn some pocket money in my early days, I used to catch moles with traps. They were then skinned and pinned out to dry on the back of the stable door. When totally dry they were then packed up and sent to Horach Friend in Wisbech, Cambridgeshire, for which we were paid an old six pence a skin. We also sent squirrel tails for which we got a bob (one shilling) a time. Both pests are with us today but not for payment.

I caught the train to Heathcoat Junior School in Tiverton at Burnhalt and travelled on the "Tivy Bumper" to and from Tiverton. To get to Burnhalt we travelled across fields at Traymill and then over a chain bridge which we enjoyed making swing to and fro. At school I have memories of playing marbles and conker competitions in the autumn. Surprisingly I passed the eleven plus exam, to go to Tiverton Grammar School, but I had to help milk the cows before I went to school. All I really wanted to do was to come home onto the farm, especially after father had purchased it. My sister and I had piano lessons, which resulted in her being good, and me forgetting every note that I had learnt. But I did enjoy playing full-back for the school rugby team, and cricket for the Stoodleigh Cavaliers. In later years, an old school mate Tony Broom, married my wife's sister Queenie and we became very good friends again.

Jan and Harry Broom stooking the sheaves.

CHAPTER FOUR
CHANGES IN FARMING LIFE

I left school in the summer of 1956; we changed our breed of cows from beef to British Friesians. Giving up hand milking, we installed a bucket milking system. I then joined Withleigh Young Farmer's Club; Jack Coombes a tenant at Prowses died and we then farmed all the land. A worker called Kelland worked for us, living with his family in the cottage. Woodwalls roof, which was thatched, needed replacing, so we got in builders from Cadbury who replaced it with galvanised iron, Father sadly got "farmer's lung" from handling old thatching reed. In 1957 we bought a new grey Ferguson tractor, and with its hydraulic system the farm became more mechanised. With this tractor, we could use a fertiliser spinner, dung spreader and mower, which speeded up work on the farm. The fertiliser spinner gave us the opportunity to sow grass seeds from it, some different from walking and using the fiddle in days gone by. My father always told me it was not time to sow fertiliser until the elm leaf was the size of an old penny. In the early 1960s compound fertiliser came more into use, which we bought from a firm called Fulfords of North Devon who also bought our wool. In those days, the wool cheque usually paid for the fertiliser, sadly today it barely pays for the shearing contractor, unless you have Devon Longwools. With the advance in machinery technology we were able to have contractors in to bale hay and straw, and in 1960 mains electricity came to the farm – no more generator problems.

In the 1960s we bought additional grass keep of 10 acres, at Penny-moor from Mr A. Guscott. He ran the local garage, there, and we continued to buy the grass keep for more than twenty years. It was not the best place to load cattle, and over the years, we experienced many difficult loadings, when cattle escaped and went in many directions, including nearly into Puddington. Interestingly we have a bill, from Mr C. G. Woodley (livestock haulier), who charged one pound to take twelve bullocks to this grass keep. In the late 1970s we were able to buy 30 acres of grass keep from Mr O. Boxall of Bickleigh Castle, and some from

Mr W. Shields at Bickleigh Mill. This field is now used annually as a maize maze. During this time we helped the Mill Farm, harvest hay crops after they had tried all the old methods of cutting and turning with horses, so that the visitors could watch with interest. I have a photo of them using oxen to carry in the bales of hay. The Bickleigh Castle ground, joined the River Exe and it flooded regularly. One year we had to move sheep, from the castle field and take them over Bickleigh Bridge and up the hill to Prowses in the dark! Then with only flashlights, we had to get them through Woodwalls Wood to the field below. All the time it tipped down with rain, and as most farmers would know, sheep do not like going through water at any time. I remember these fields at the castle when I was a child, that when the river flooded rabbits would go to all the high points of the meadows, and we used to take our Springer Spaniel down to retrieve them (this being prior to Myxomatosis when there were hundreds more rabbits around).

I met my wife to be, Jeannette in 1959. In 1962 we became engaged at Christmas, and after heavy snow on Boxing Day, we did not see each other until mid February. During this period two Dartmoor prisoners escaped, and were recaptured in our lower orchard, because their footprints made it easy for the police dogs to follow their escape. In 1964 Jan (Jeannette) and I married, and lived the Rectory flat in Bickleigh. We rented an additional fourteen acres of Glebe land in Bickleigh, which allowed us to increase our sheep flock, buying from markets on Exmoor (Anstey and Raleighs Cross). At Bickleigh we built two poultry houses, and began a Christmas turkey enterprise which continued for the next thirty years. Interestingly we started with Broad Breasted Bronze, and then Dimple Whites, but now the most popular fresh turkey is a Dimple Bronze, which shows fashion goes round in a circle.

Meanwhile we were trying to get planning for a bungalow at Way Farm, which was held up mainly by an inadequate water supply. This was eventually overcome and we moved approximately four years later into a Woolaway bungalow which cost £2,200 erected, which was sold in 2003 to be taken away for £4,400 to rebuild. In 1966 my sister Margaret married a farmer's son from Upton-Pyne – John Leach who worked at Stonemans, a tractor and machinery business. My sister worked in the laboratory in Exeter Hospital. In this year I bought a new tractor from John, and mower. After his move to Dorset when he was working for South West Farmers and Bredy Supplies, he sold us a combine and a second hand parlour which was fitted into the old root house, giving us the opportunity to milk

Above: *My wedding at Cullompton.*

Left: *My father and mother at my wedding.*

Below: *Father winning first prize with cattle at Tiverton Junction market*

six cows at any one time. Upon moving to Dorset my sister became a teacher until 1992, when she had to give up teaching and became a Registrar of Births, Marriages and Deaths.

In 1968 our milk was collected from us, from a bulk tank, we being the first in our area to go bulk. We expanded the dairy herd to over fifty cows, and erected a silage barn, slurry store, and feeding area in Lower Spot. At this time we started a system of herd health with our local vet Alan Hopkins; once a month he visited and checked cows for health problems, feet problems and whether they were in calf. Our daughter Sally was born in 1965, followed by Wendy in 1967 and Julie in 1971. In 1970, I was elected parish councillor for Bickleigh, but after three years I decided that I had had enough. In the early 1970s Britain was invaded by Dutch elm disease – this is a beetle that destroys the bark of the tree so eventually the tree dies. This spread through the elm trees on our farms and all of them had to be cut down. The Elm still grows in our hedges to about fifteen feet tall, then sadly succumbs to the beetle. It has been said that if all elms were cut to the ground and burnt, the beetles could not survive and the elm tree would return to the countryside. Quite a few beams in Way Farm house and buildings were made from elm because they were straight and looked to a good finish when they were cleaned up. When you travel the roads of Britain some of our hedges look very dilapidated with dead elms, which die off after eight to ten years growth and look very untidy. The loss of the English elm was one of the biggest losses that the woodland industry has had to face but there is hope that a new strain of elm will become resistant before too long.

In 1972, we bought 44 acres of River Exe meadows, from the Castle Estate, 13 acres was purchased at 300 pounds an acre (privately), followed by 31 acres at 500 pounds an acre after auction. We sold Prowses and 36 acres at 600 pounds an acre. For 180 pounds we bought a second hand Dutch barn, which we erected in the new fields. In 1973, Jan, the family and I started our annual holidays to Padstow, North Cornwall until 2004 and for over ten years we owned a chalet in St Merryn. In 1973 when major works were made to Bickleigh Bridge, stone was taken from our quarry to use as it was said to match the existing stone construction well; probably the stone came from our quarry which was used on the original bridge. Also, when major repairs were made to St Peter's church in Tiverton, two or three loads of shaped quality stone from Woodwalls were used to repair the tower.

The date 1976 will always be remembered as being drought year, when we made very low yields of silage and corn, but it was followed by a mild winter – nature always takes care of itself! This was also the year that we moved into the old farm house, and mother and father moved into the bungalow opposite. In the winter of 1978 we had the first snow and blizzards since 1962, and we had to take our milk to tankers on the main roads, but one day John Henson from Cadbury and I took our milk to Crediton in emergency tanks. The roads had not been cleared of snow, and near the gateways it was piled six to eight feet deep! After struggling at times we arrived at the lorry store to find that all the lorries were full of milk, so we had to wait six hours to unload our milk – our journey took all day! In the winter of 1982 we had to take the milk to Bickleigh Bridge for several days. In the summer whilst cutting grass at Woodwalls, I had one moment's lack of concentration on very steep ground; I tipped the tractor and mower over. The safety cab saved my life, but meant we had to get a contractor to upright the tractor, and the experience left me very shaken, but relieved. In 1979 we bought our first four-wheel-drive tractor, a Deutz. We held a silage demonstration organised by Witheridge Garage and my brother in law.

In 1981 Sally left school to work on the farm, as father's health deteriorated. We milked sixty cows, and had the first computerisation on the farm, when we fitted Out of Parlour feeders. This gave a huge saving in that we did not have to handle cow cake in bags, and gave an excellent control of feeding the cows to their milk yield. This also helped us pick out cows that were unwell, or on heat, when they did not eat their prescribed amount of feed. Whilst John Leach was working as the Deutz sales manager for the UK he took us on a tour of their factory in Germany. In 1984, when John became sales manager Fendt UK we bought a 304 plus loader, after a demonstration of reseeding on the side of our steeper fields. In the 1980s we needed to re-thatch part of the farm house, so to save costs we grew several acres of special variety of wheat (Maris Widgeon) on which you could not sow any nitrogen fertiliser because it weakens the strengthen of the reed. The task of cutting with a binder and stooking it for a couple of weeks is a very hard working job; you then have to carry it and store it until the reed comber is available and it takes about ten men to complete this task. We grew more reed wheat for several years and the quality of it is determined by the weather at that time. Nowadays thatchers prefer imported water reed from the likes of Hungary and Poland. Our thatchers were the Hannabus family from Plymtree in Devon. At this time Harry Broom, a retired farm worker from Burn, started working at Way for half a day a week. He was one of the old school farm workers, enjoying hedging, cleaning out houses and ditches etc. He was not happy unless he was working for most of the daylight hours, making a first class job of everything he encountered. He worked for

The milking buildings in Lower Spot.

Transporting milk to tanker in 1982.

Thatching Way Farm house.

Bindering wheat in the valley.

Demonstrations.

us until his health and eyesight deteriorated.

In 1987 Sally married Richard Reed from Plymtree. Father became quite ill at this time and we took the decision to sell the cows because of the pollution risk in Lower Spot which was so close to the River Exe. The risk of polluting was extremely great, and as I had become a Magistrate I was fully aware of the huge financial penalty which followed a successful prosecution. In 1987 the unpredicted hurricane blew down many trees, and took the galvanised roof off Woodwalls barn. In 1988, my daughter Wendy married Keith Kerslake, in the same year my dear father died in October after a long illness. We shut down the buildings in Lower Spot and sold them for reuse. In 1990 we built a large shed, the site work and construction being well completed by the Luffman family. For two years, we bought and sold freshly calved heifers until we saw there was not enough profit in it so we changed gradually into a suckler herd.

From when we were married, for over 36 years, we reared and sold Christmas turkeys and geese. We had our own regular band of helpers, who included Mrs Ivy Broom, Mrs Coombes – the widow of the last tenant of Prowses – and both sides of our families. We usually reared around 250 turkeys, and ten geese. About 120 turkeys, and the geese, went as private orders, the rest were bought by local butchers. All the preparation for sale took around a week, and by Christmas we were all pretty tired, but it did help to supplement the income. In the early days, turkey was a special dish at Christmas, but now is available all year round. Instead goose is more of a traditional meal at Christmas.

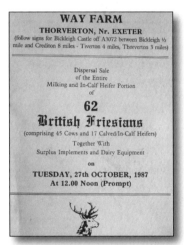

Cow sale 1987.

Silage demonstration by Witheridge Garage.

Guarding new trees at Woodwalls.

Tree planting at Woodwalls by tractor.

CHAPTER FIVE

CHANGES TO THE FARM 1988-

W̲e had a couple of traumatic years, with the loss of my father and two daughters married, and the other daughter off to catering college at Slough to make her own way in life. We sold the dairy herd and concentrated on Friesian heifers, which we bought as mostly three to four month old heifers from private and farm sales. This unfortunately brought problems with disease, freemartins, and some sadly in calf at twelve months old. After struggling for a couple of years, we put all our heifers on to a Hereford bull so we could change to a suckler herd. In 1991 we bought suckler cows from Dartmoor and from Bill Speak from North Tawton; we bought a Charolais bull and two cows and calves from a breeder at Whitstone. Our bull had the nickname of Bimbo. In starting this herd we aimed to sell the calves at nine months old at South Molton market. In 1992 I unfortunately had to have a left ankle fusion, because the bones in my foot had become displaced. I was in plaster for three months, and my salvation was that David Leach bought a quad bike for me, at a charity auction. It came with a trailer which was used extensively, for carrying ewes and lambs, to fields after lambing. In 1995 Way Farm, Trey Mill Farm and Bidwell Farm went down in quick succession with tuberculosis and sadly we lost twenty-five cattle in thirteen months before coming clear. MAFF decided to cull badgers and in three months, a hundred and thirty-five were caught, of which forty percent had tuberculosis, some with very visible signs. At this time we could not sell any stock other than straight to the abattoir; we had therefore a lot more stock than normal. MAFF advised us to raise all our feeders and water troughs so that badgers could not infect the drinking water and feed. We also fenced off our black barn, so that no badgers could get in with the cattle and feed. After six months sadly we had more reactors and lost further cattle. After my ankle fusion it was not easy to work to my full potential, so with the TB episode we took the decision to take out some of the steep land, and plant hardwood trees. This was encouraged, because we had recently jointly won the Otter trophy for conservation in Devon. In

Foot and mouth lambs to skip.

A picture of children and grandchildren.

Five generations of family.

1998 when we at last were free from TB another decision was made to sell the suckler herd privately. At this time we bought a bale wrapper and for the next few years annually wrapped and stacked roughly 4000 bales of silage for neighbours. My cousin Alan Isaac did the baling with a Claas baler. Our interest in planting trees became greater *(see part two, chapter four)*. I also became involved with Radio Devon, *(see part two, chapter two)*. With the extended tree planting plus two new ponds, our interest in wild flowers and wildlife became more satisfying, because we were being paid a subsidy to plant and look after the trees. In 1999 we entered the Devon wild flowers competition, winning prize money of £500 and dug our first sizable pond in the moor. In 2000, at Woodwalls we planted 21 acres of trees, and two more ponds. At this time my cousin Alan bought the Lamb Inn in Silverton, so he gave up baling and we stopped stacking and wrapping, which was a relief from travelling miles and working late at night.

2001 was sad for me because I lost a great friend, Edwin Cole of Witheridge. Edwin and I had been group leaders of the Tiverton YFC, for several years and went to Denmark together on the scholarship trip. After his death, I became very friendly with his brother Cyril at Rose Ash – he has been very influential in helping water divine our ponds, and encourage our wild-flower meadows.

February 2001 saw one of the most distressing times for farmers this country has ever known. Foot and Mouth disease was brought to Devon from a Northern market in a lorry load of sheep. There were many outbreaks in Devon, with huge burning piles of carcases. The smell not only from the fires, but from rotting carcases was a disgrace to animal health in this country. DEFRA, now the successor of MAFF was very slow in bringing it under control. There were millions of pounds wasted in condemning meat, which was in no way having any contact with FMD. DEFRA was too slow in shutting down markets, and the disease spread rapidly. The nearest outbreaks to us, were at Crediton and just outside Tiverton. At this time, we had 200 fat lambs ready for slaughter, but they were taken away only to be put in a skip and burnt. Information at this time was hopeless. I rang DEFRA after a flood warning, asking permission to move my sheep from the river meadows to higher ground; they told me that I could not, unless I gave three days notice. This was absolutely ridiculous as I was prepared to disinfect eight feet of minor highway to save my sheep from drowning. I rang the National Farmers Union and eventually a ministry vet, rang me to give me permission to remove them ASAP, but had no idea of my location. He was given my holding number, but went on to ask me whereabouts in Okehampton did I live. I told him, I did not realise that the River Exe was anywhere near Okehampton! In another phone call made to DEFRA the gentleman on the end of the phone could not find Exeter on his map, and did not know what "yew's" (ewes) were, he told me to ring the NFU! All shows were cancelled this year except Devon County Show was held in August with no livestock. The outbreak went on into November before brought under control, this was an extremely harrowing and lonely time for farmers, who stayed at home, to prevent the risk of spreading the disease, all markets and even weddings were postponed.

In 2002, I accidently swallowed kerosene whilst siphoning some for mother's Rayburn; this led to me having serious pneumonia and I spent a month in the Royal Devon and Exeter Hospital. During this time, we had to sell one-hundred Dorset sheep, that were due to lamb: it was impossible for Jan to look after them as when I came out hospital I was unable to work for a period of six weeks. During 2002 my mum was taken

very ill, and for some time we had realised she was suffering from some
form of Dementia.

Living with Dementia and Addison's

Dear mum had suffered with Addison's disease for twenty years, which is
an underactive thyroid; it is a rare disorder in which symptoms are caused
by a deficiency of the costeroid hormones. Normally produced by the
adrenal glands, it was fatal before hormone treatment became available in
late 1950s. Without the necessary drugs, she would go into a form of
unconsciousness and when she was first diagnosed by one of our local
doctors, who had luckily seen it before, she had become seriously ill. It was
controlled by drugs, but if she had a sickness or infection, and she could
not absorb the drugs, she would quickly lose control of her mental
functions. Over the years we had found her in this state on numerous
occasions and needed hospital medical attention urgently. With this condition it probably took us longer for us to realise that in her early eighties
we were seeing signs of confusion in her life. She also had regular blood
tests and visits to the consultant. After a period of time, we realised she
was probably not taking her full quota of pills per day or in the correct
order. Mum had always done her own medication for years, with little
problem. After huge persuasion we got her to use a daily tablet container,
so we could monitor it. She was not happy that Jan checked it out daily, but
in time Jan had to take full control of her medication. She became confused
as to which day of the week it was, and at my sister Margaret's for her
eightieth birthday she was not fully aware of what we were all celebrating.
It was difficult to persuade friends and family that something was wrong
and you had to be with her twenty-four hours a day to see the early signs
of dementia. She seemed to put on a front when she had short term visitors.

The following incidents are probably relevant. At times she would
dress with her underclothes on top, and when told her answer was
normally "nothing's wrong, I'm not expecting anyone". She would come
knocking on the farmhouse door in the middle of the night, asking for
bread for breakfast, time meant nothing to her. She would ask to be taken
to church in mid week and if you did not agree she would threaten to walk.
She came down to lunch one Sunday at the farmhouse and locked herself
in the upstairs toilet. We tried for some considerable time to persuade her
to unlock the door. Eventually I had to get a ladder and crawl across a
plastic roof, and through a window. On entry, mum shouted "There's a

man coming in the window!" On one early morning visit to the bungalow I was met by a huge amount of smoke in the kitchen; she had put a newspaper on the top of the hot plates and turned them on, instead of the toaster. I opened the window and threw the burning paper outside. Her sister Chris used to bring dinner for her on Mondays but we frequently saw her giving it to the dogs. She always wanted to go for a ride in the car, even when I was going to court, and it was difficult to stop her from getting in. We used to leave the car at the bottom of the lane so she would not notice that I was leaving. A visit to Plymouth was difficult, for by this time she was having incontinence problems. We were astounded as she quickly went into the men's toilet, and eventually Jan had to tidy her up. Normally mum was very neat and tidy (as a child I always had to wash behind my ears!), but she wore clothes over and over again, and her lack of personal cleanliness was noticeable. I or Jan monitored her regularly during the day, trying not for her to see us.

In September 2002 she had another Addison's crisis and went to the Royal Devon and Exeter Hospital. Early next morning the hospital rang, to say she had taken a turn for the worse, and was unlikely to live for much longer. I rang Margaret and we stayed with her all day, as medics gave her their full attention. That night there was no change in her condition, so we were advised to go home, and they would call if her condition worsened. Next morning's visit was a surprise. She was sitting up in bed, very confused and her comment was "I spose you thought I snuffed it". The next few visits were difficult to absorb. Her mind led her to believe that bicycles were at the bottom of the bed, her doctor's surgery was in the ceiling and that she knew all the other people in the next beds to her as well. She had a phobia of trying to make holes in blankets, or folding them up, at times she would try to remove my shoes, for her to put on. She thought at one time she was going to the Devon County Show, and said "All those people over there are queued up for the County Show, I'll go join them".

Eventually she was transferred to Tiverton Hospital where I was regularly introduced to the staff as her husband Bill. She insisted that she could go home and look after herself, but the home visit was a disaster. She put a metal plate in the microwave – it was her first time using it. She was moved from Tiverton to St Lawrence's Crediton, which is a monitoring unit to see how she could cope. On her first day there, she went missing, and was spotted by Jan's cousin's wife, Audrey Tucker, walking down to the town intending to catch a bus anywhere it took her. After a conference with doctors it was decided she should be transferred to the Confused Unit at Crediton, and undergo a brain scan, at Exeter. The scan showed she had had minor strokes affecting her brain, and so was kept in Exeter Hospital for a while. She was sent back to Crediton, but it was obvious she was deteriorating fast. Visits to her were getting very difficult for all of us, especially Margaret who saw her every week and had a long journey home to Weymouth which was a two hour trip one way. Sometimes on visits she would play "musical chairs", continually on the move and not communicating. Sometimes I would have to go for a walk around the farm after a visit to clear my mind. To all extent mum was lost to us as we knew her, and we now know we were grieving for her long before her death. The staff at Crediton Hospital were fantastic, with sympathetic caring, for mum and us. They will never know how their words to us helped us through this difficult time. We needed to visit our only mum, but were very apprehensive before each visit.

Mum continued to have minor strokes, and eventually died in May 2003. We were spared twenty-four hour care of someone with Addison's and Alzheimer's but can sympathise with the many celebrities that have gone public with their own experiences, and what great help this gives to those living with the same problems. Just talking about it, gives most comfort from the strain of living with Dementia.

2004-

After Margaret found our lost relations in Canada, Jan, Queenie, Tony and I organised a month's stay in Canada. We stayed a week with Barry Greenslade and his family. A farewell meal felt like the whole family was reunited, a truly emotional gathering. We let the grass keep, and arable land was farmed by Richard Reed, my son-in-law. During this time, I started to experience bad kidney stone problems, and was continually in and out of hospital. We sold the old Woolaway bungalow and had plans passed for a replacement retirement bungalow, as I had now become an OAP. Consultation with our architect Richard Sellers provided a bungalow with a difference, high ceilings in the kitchen and living room, with glorious window views over the Exe Valley. Builder Peter Wainwright and his team proved to be first class builders who consulted with us during construction. He also advised us on minor but enhancing alterations. I was able to help as "builders' mate", and after Jan's initial fears of how small it looked, it became clear it would be of adequate size. We put in a staircase

Above: *BBC filming bore hole construction.*

Left: *Our new home.*

Below left: *Fendt tractor re-seeding steep fields.*

Below right: *Digging one of the seven ponds.*

to utilise space above the bedrooms, which was used as a workroom upstairs. Then came the garden construction, and landscaping plus two small ponds close to house. During this year we also planted a small acreage of hardwood trees. 2006 saw me continually having kidney stone problems, when I paid an unfruitful visit to Bristol Hospital to remove a nine millimetre stone from my kidney. They told my consultant it was gone, but two months later, he had to operate and remove the stone at the Royal Devon and Exeter Hospital. 2007 saw us win a gold medal for our woodlands at the Devon County Show. This year was an extremely wet year, when many one day shows were cancelled due to waterlogged ground. The year also saw us travel to New Zealand, a country I had always wanted to visit. It was not exactly how I expected to find it: the North Island was very volcanic, but some very impressive trees. One night we stayed on a farm, which kept 100 Angus cattle on fifty acres, but different to us, grass grew 365 days a year. The South Island was very dry and humid, and we saw many new vineyards being created. Only on the Canterbury Plains did we see any very green fields. A lovely country with superb hospitality, but I still think I prefer my visit to Canada.

The year 2008 did not start well, with further kidney stone operations, at the Bristol and Exeter hospitals, followed by a prostate, which after the operation meant no work for eight weeks. Stone problems continued so my doctor sent me to Guy's Hospital where eventually in August I was operated on, and after fresh medication all is still well. That summer again was wet – is it because of thirteen new moons in the year? At Devon County Show, we won the Woodland Trust Trophy, as well as silver medal for one piece of woodland. The world shearing contest was held in Norway in October, and we took the chance of a short visit and experienced a small taste of Norway. 2009 brought continuing success in Devon County Show woodland competitions where we won another gold medal and retained the Woodland Trust Trophy. Our wildflowers were exceptionally good this year, and more and more people came on our bluebell walks, in aid of the Children's Hospice South West charity. In June 2009, we went to Finland for ten days, on an organised trip. We went into the arctic circle, and travelled through Lapland, visiting a reindeer farm. Finland, was much more level than I anticipated but we were not surprised to see so many trees and lakes. What did surprise us, was that at their town markets they sold numerous strawberries, and green peas in pods. The northern half of Finland has more modern buildings, as all the buildings including churches, were destroyed by the Germans in World War II. Their military cemeteries were kept in immaculate order. In Finland in June, it was totally light for twenty four hours a day and the sun never set, while in winter it never becomes light. Nevertheless a very interesting country to visit.

As I look back over the years, the advance of technology on farms, has moved at a tremendous pace. The advances that affect me directly, are, firstly, the invention of the electric fencer, which has allowed farmers to contain stock and stripfeed root crops – used as an alternative to the dreaded barbed wire, it is now one thing that most livestock farmers cannot live without. Then came the Big Baler, which has allowed us to change our plans when making hay. When rain is forecast earlier than suspected, we can now bale and wrap into haylage or silage round bales, avoiding spoiling the crop. With straw, one can bale and leave in the field for days, whatever the weather, because the rain just runs off the side, without penetrating the bale.

The computerisation of feeding and milking systems, has transformed the dairy industry. No longer do we have to handle bags of cake, but now bulk bins are used on most dairy farms, with out of parlour feeding systems computerised to feed individual cows a prescribed amount of cake. Our first tractor was a Standard Fordson, of about 30 horse power and cost father £55 second hand. When we bought our first four wheel drive tractor, it cost £7000 and my father remarked "That's more than I paid for the farm!" Most tractors today are between 100 and 200 horsepower, costing between £20,000 and £50,000. A self propelled forester, is far in excess of £100,000, but both of these implements have such versatility in their use. The flail hedge trimmer, has revolutionised the way our hedges are kept, but must be used yearly, by a knowledgeable operator. In the field we have seen the development of much better yielding corn varieties, giving a much better return. The countryside is certainly more colourful when the yellow flower of rape is in flower in the spring. More and more maize has been grown in the last few years, proving to be an excellent feed for livestock. Crops of potatoes, and Devon swedes are grown under plastic covers, whilst more fruit is now grown in plastic tunnels.

Livestock, both cattle and sheep, has changed too, with many continental breeds now bred on our Devon farms, but some of the old breeds of sheep, such as the Devon Closewool, Exmoor Horn and Greyfaced Dartmoor are best suited the moors in our county. The Devon and South Devon cattle play an important part in the hills, and have maintained their numbers.

Another important machine on most farms is the quad bike which has led to a better way of seeing and herding livestock, certainly better then walking in the old days! My father had a saying that "second class riding was better than first class walking!". The quad acts as another dog that can never be replaced, especially on the moorlands of Dartmoor and Exmoor.

During this period of time, I have been fortunate to have had an addition of five wonderful grandchildren, Steven Reed born in 1989, Laura Reed in 1991, Alex Kerslake in 1993, Jess Kerslake 1994, and finally in 2008 Abbie Millington (an Irish grand daughter). All give me great pleasure in latter years.

Since 1988 and our reduction in livestock, my wife Jan has taken up painting landscapes in oil for which she has a natural talent. She paid a visit to her cousin Gerry Hillman, who is a well known West County artist and has created many pictures which adorn our bungalow. She is an ardent gardener who is also on the local garden club committee. For many years she has taught children from Bickleigh School to swim as well as being a school governor for 13 years. But hasn't Bickleigh village changed over the last twenty years! It has lost its resident parson, a bakery and shop, and there is no longer a policeman living in the village; but we have now have a railway centre at the old Cadeleigh Station and a craft centre at the Old Mill and quite a few holiday cottages.

One can only wonder what changes lie ahead, in the next twenty years.

YFC County Chairman 1966.

CHAPTER SIX

THE YOUNG FARMER'S EXPERIENCE

Little did I realise, that joining a Young Farmers Club would have such a huge influence in my life. The old motto of "Good farmer, Good countryman, Good citizen", has led me in many directions of my life. I first joined the Tiverton Grammar School YFC in 1952. We had an allotment and two hives of bees at school, where Mr "Flash" White was the leader, and I tended the bees with his help. In all we had about ten members, the rest growing vegetables for the school. Leaving school I joined Withleigh YFC and the first meeting was at the TIverton Memorial Hall, and its members came from within a five mile radius. Herbert Twose was the club leader who gave me good advice, which was the more you put into the club the more you will get in return. He was a strong advocate of proficiency tests, and Withleigh club had national recognition for having the first two members to obtain Mastercraft badges in England (Margaret Lear, Mavis Kerslake) and the first boy to win a gold Farmcraft badge was John Kerslake. I in time passed Turfhedging, Machine Milking, Ploughing, Sheep Shearing, Gate Making, Stockman's Task, Butter making, Stone Walling and Root Singling, which culminated in me winning a gold award in 1963.

W. R. Wilson M B E

The club was one of over fifty clubs in the Devon Federation and at that time Mr "Tug" Wilson was County Organiser. Tug was known throughout the whole YFC movement and especially for his famous whiskers, red waistcoat, and wooden leg. He was inspirational in his work within the Devon YFC movement, and he helped many members to represent their county at national Stockjudging and Public Speaking competitions and encouraged people to apply for international exchange visits. He was one of the original committee that set up the world Golden Shears Competition which is now a regular global attraction, showing the very best in machine and blade shearing and wool handling. Tug's ashes are actually scattered at the shearing stand at Bath and West showground in Shepton Mallet. Tug was a stickler for timing, in all competitions being there early to book teams in for individual competitions. Devon YFC should be proud of his service to the movement, being recognised by being awarded an MBE and I for one will always be grateful to him to his help when I was a county officer.

Public Speaking with Tug Wilson.

Good Farmer

The education that Withleigh YFC provided to members was mostly through proficiency tests. Other educational events were trips to the London Dairy Show, BOCM Mills at Bristol, the Buckfastleigh Wool Factory, the Fatstock Show at Smithfield in London and Liscombe Experimental Farm on Exmoor, to name just a few. These trips were very enjoyable, because of the humorous activities of Dennis Rabjohns in particular. On the return journey from London on one trip, in the dark he handed

THE DEVON COUNTY FEDERATION OF YOUNG FARMERS CLUBS

14th February, 1964

This is to certify that John Greenslade has been awarded the John Spear Memorial Travel Scholarship.

W.R. Wilson.

John Spear Award 1967 (first winner).

around Quality Street chocolates, which had all the various wrappers, but inside was actually a nub of cow cake! On another occasion he and an accomplice John Middleton, walked across Piccadilly carrying a hurricane lantern. The old Tiverton Show was a yearly event which involved many members, within the Tiverton group of YFCs. Withleigh regularly won the Roller Mills Cup on many occasions. Withleigh YFC was founded in 1929 by Lord Amory, Harold Shapland and others as a calf club, which as years went by, developed into calf, sheep and pig keeping. Every year there was a Show and Sale of the stock. I kept beef cattle and sheep at various times, and actually won the sheep championship one year. Sadly now, proficiency tests have stopped while the agricultural colleges have taken on the work and training on the farm. A new skill is being able to fill in the volume of paperwork provided to farmers from DEFRA; we also have Skills for Life now in our club programme. The speaking competitions vary from quiz, junior public speaking, brains trust to public speaking, mostly based on countryside topics. It is important to train young people to be able to speak up for the countryside. Regular exchange visits are made to various YFCs within Great Britain. I participated in some in my time, visiting Romsey in Hampshire and Rhea Valley in Shropshire.

Good Countryman

Young Farmers are first class ambassadors for the countryside when travelling overseas, which many of our members have done. Many countries have been visited and on their return they give talks and slideshows on their trip. Many members have also gone on to become Parish and County Councillors. YFC members have done various projects in the community during difficult times. I remember helping to man footpaths on the Devon, Somerset border during a Foot and Mouth outbreak in 1967, to try to stop the disease entering Devon. All cars and especially lorries had disinfectant used on their wheels, and we manned during the night whilst NFU members did it by day. We have also helped lamb sheep for a farmer at Oakford, who was seriously ill at the time. Whilst in Withleigh YFC, I became a vice chairman in 1961, and in following year I became chairman. I was very proud to become chairman of such a prestigious club, and became very involved in all the competitions that the club had on offer. In 1964 I was the first winner of the John Spear Memorial Scholarship, in which I won a trip to Denmark. I travelled with members from throughout the county who had applied and won a place on this trip. In this year I also became an assistant club leader, becoming a joint club leader in the years 1965 to 1970. I represented the club on the county executive committee and surprise, surprise in 1964 I was elected county junior vice chairman. I well remember representing Withleigh at the national AGM in London when Michael Lear and I paid our first visit to the capital. The Devon contingent stayed at the Regent Palace Hotel. Leaving the train at Waterloo Station, and reaching street daylight we were brought to the reality of the rush and hustle of the city of London. Everyone seemed to be in such a hurry, and the walk to the hotel was a dodgems experience particularly as we were carrying our cases. It was a luxurious hotel, with every facility. Two years later, I was honoured to propose a motion at the AGM that all proficiency gold badge winners should be presented with scrolls, which was agreed by all.

When I became county chairman I was the third to come from the Withleigh club, and this involved attending many meetings. The Devon Federation, at this time appointed Tanner Shields as Tug Wilson's assistant. Tanner and I became good friends and later on he became the National Secretary of YFC. Whilst being county chairman, I was privileged to visit many of the fifty clubs in Devon. Usually I was asked to speak at the club's AGM, Harvest Supper or judge some competitions. This experience led me to meet many members during this time, and some of us still recognise and converse with each other today! We manage to prise the county rally away after many years at Exeter market, and take it around all parts of the county. I was extremely proud to have been chairman of such a leading YFC county, and in 1967 was asked to receive the national competitions cup at the AGM. Thank you YFC, for giving me one of the proudest moments in my life. YFC is well known to be a marriage bureau. I was no exception and met my wife at a Whimple YFC function. In 1969 I became the Tiverton group chairman, and hosted at times various international exchangees. I remember especially Ross Wisneski from New Zealand, who was staying with us, when Neil Armstrong landed on the moon; we corresponded for some time after his return. In 1980 the Devon YFC federation made me a life vice president of Devon YFC.

Good Citizen

The YFC raises thousands of pounds for many local and national charities. In 1981 I was elected president of Withleigh YFC, and in my final year as president I was heavily involved with a memorial walk, with Ian Botham

Walking with Ian Botham on a stage of his John o'Groats to Lands End.

Funding thanks from Exeter Hospital.

in raising money for leukaemia research. Earlier that year I had been training a junior public speaking team, who made it all the way to the national finals. Elizabeth Webber was a sixteen year old girl from Whimple who was the top speaker at the final in which the team came second. Just two weeks after this event, she was diagnosed with leukaemia. Sadly even after a marrow bone transplant, she lost her fight to beat the disease and in her memory the Tiverton YFC and Honiton YFC groups, got together to raise £5000 for a freezing unit for bone marrow transplants at the Royal Devon and Exeter Hospital. Every conceivable way of raising this huge sum, was ventured. I opened the fund, by raising £1000 on my walk from Wellington to Cadbury, obtaining sponsorship from many of my farming friends and neighbours. This joint effort amazed us all, by raising a total of nearly £11,000, so we presented the children's ward at Royal Devon and Exeter Hospital with many extra gifts for which the YFC movement won much praise. Withleigh held an annual whist drive to raise money for local charities, at which I was the master of ceremonies for several years. YFCs have contributed time and effort to things like tidying the garden at Tidcombe Hall, landscaping the garden at the old Heathcoat Community Centre, and we made and presented a Christmas Crib to St Peter's Church Tiverton, in 1963. In 1965 I was asked by the East Devon College if I would visit Exeter Prison, to talk to a group of twenty prisoners. This experience led me never to want to spend time, in this establishment. A funny experience in my memory was when the club entered a pram race from Bampton to Tiverton. We needed a pram, which was offered to us from a farm across the valley. Andrew Tapp and I went to collect it, but on arrival we found out that the pram was in use, to move dung from the parlour to the dung heap, and therefore needed a total washout! In the 1960s Withleigh YFC became involved with many other youth organisations in Tiverton, leading to heavy involvement in the special events of the Tiverton youth week. Many other examples of YFC good citizenship are remembered with pride.

Withleigh YFC 75th Anniversary with four Devon County Ex -Chairmen.

Planting trees at West Point with previous County Chairmen.

Conclusion of YFC

I do not think I can ever repay, the debt I owe to the YFC movement it has given me confidence, skills, education and the opportunity meet so many people, at club, group, county and national level. Good friendships have been forged over many years and it is good to see young members excel in all club activities. In 2002 Withleigh came second in the national final of Club of Year. 2009 was a tremendous year when the club won the group, county, and South-West area finals of the Pantomime competition. They became second in the national Southern finals, and the enthusiasm of all the members was there to see with total enjoyment, which is something that YFC is all about. This was also the year when Withleigh YFC celebrated 80 years of continuous success as a YFC club, with a dinner and dance at the Tiverton Motel. Over the past 80 years a handful of people have become county chairman, Roger Hill, Jenny Rabjohns, Les Heywood and myself, whilst Jenny Rabjohns went on to become national chairman – what a record! It has been a privilege to have been a member of Withleigh Young Farmers Club to which many members have given and received such success. Long may it continue.

68

PART TWO

THE
OTHER
SIDE OF
LIFE

Receiving my twenty years Long Service Award.

CHAPTER SEVEN
TWENTY YEARS EXPERIENCE
OF A MAGISTRATE

Never had it crossed my mind, or had I ever thought about becoming a magistrate until the 1980s, when a friend of Young Farmers days, Albert Cook and I were judging a speaking competition in North Devon. We had judged several times together, and I always admired his calm and extremely well-thought-out opinions. We had also worked together in sheep shearing competitions, he being a respected senior judge of national recognition, and at this time he was the chairman of the South Molton Bench. He tentatively asked me if I was interested in becoming a magistrate on several occasions. My reply was always that milking cows did not give me enough time to give it justice (excuse the pun!). He was emphatic that all sections of society should be on the Bench including farmers. When in 1987 we sold the dairy herd, he immediately invited me to a day at South Molton to see a court in action. Albert told me that a Mr John Persey (Farmer) was retiring at Cullompton and he was prepared to give me every help to apply to replace him. In due time, I applied and was called to an interview at the Court House in Cullompton. Sadly at this time, my father had become extremely ill and I had been up with him most of the night prior to the interview. I was met at the court by the Clerk to the Bench, Andrew Mimmack. After being given some scenarios to read I was then interviewed by three magistrates. One scenario was about a burglary where the intruder had ransacked the house but had also urinated on the carpet. After being asked what action should be taken, I remember saying that the defendant as well as being fined heavily, should pay for a new carpet. I came away not too confident especially as Albert was not able to appraise me, because of our friendship.

Time elapsed until the 25th of July 1989; I received news from the Lord Chancellor about my appointment to the Cullompton Bench. On the 10th of August I was sworn in, at Cullompton and met other members of this

Bench; Francis Welland (an accountant) was also sworn in at the same time. Jan was invited to see this event when Lord Morley, representing the Queen, performed the ceremony. There were two oaths. The first oath of allegiance reads "I swear by Almighty God, that I will be faithful and bear true allegiance to Her Majesty Queen Elizabeth the Second, Her Heirs and Successors according to law." The judicial oath is "I swear by Almighty God, that I well and truly serve our Sovereign Lady, Queen Elizabeth the Second in the office of Justice of the Peace and I will do right to all manner of people, after the laws and usages of this realm, without fear or favour, affection or ill will."

The Chairman of the Bench at Cullompton was Cecil Stoneman, a council member of Halberton Parish Council, who worked for the Water Board. Other members of the Bench were John Maunder of Lloyd Maunder, Willand, Mrs Ann Walter a domestic science teacher, Mrs Helen Lancaster a caterer of Culmstock, Mr Arthur Williams an insurance broker from Silverton. In addition there was Mrs Hazel Mckinnel a dentist's wife from Bradninch, Professor Malyn Newitt a university lecturer from Plymtree, Mrs Jean Cooper an electrician's wife from Halberton, Mrs Jill Bent a holiday home owner and finally Ian Cummings a nurseryman from Cullompton.

A weekend's training course followed at Dartington College, when I went with Geoff Clapp who had been appointed to the Tiverton Bench. Court day at Cullompton was normally a Monday where there were two courts: the main bigger court dealt with mostly criminal and motoring matters, whilst the smaller court was involved in non-police matters, overweight lorries, TV licences and car tax evasion etc. In those days we were sent our court lists through the post and knew who we would be sitting with on that day. We were known as the M5 motorway court for Devon – 80% of motoring offences came before us from the M5. My first sitting was with Court Chairman Cecil Stoneman and I had an early baptism, when we sent an offender to prison for three months. The powers of detention that we had then struck home, and I admit I worried a little about it afterwards. But Cecil told me "Don't take court business home with you", very good advice from a superb chairman who showed authority, compassion and reality when needed. After two years I was able to take the chair, starting with afternoon sittings when only paperwork was dealt with. Cecil gave me the opportunity to take the chair on a more regular basis. I also joined the Youth Bench which sat every fortnight on a Wednesday, alternating jointly with the Tiverton Bench. There were times when we were invited to sit at the Crown Court at the Castle Exeter on sentencing matters, which was a whole different experience sitting with a professional judge. Memories of one judge who regularly had his black labrador in his Chambers, another who on retiring always saw it necessary to light a cigar. Now we only sit on appeals at the new Crown Court, Southernhay Gardens and the wigged barristers and the different style of judges make it a whole new experience. At the Castle there was a maze of corridors and steps whereas the new court is ultra-modern with little natural light. On two occasions I visited Plymouth Crown Court following a case of a drug addict and thief who wished to reform. He gave up his drug addiction but sadly was unable to stop his theft of cars. Cullompton was a friendly Bench and it gave me the opportunity to meet and work with people of many different occupations. In the eleven years I sat at Cullompton those that were appointed were a pharmacist, silver expert, ex-head teacher, ex-service officer, a registrar and an accountant. At Tiverton Youth Court I sat with a store business owner, bank manager, lorry body builder, nurse, hairdresser and a nursing home owner. Tiverton Court was held in the Town Hall Chambers, not the best court room in Devon by a long shot, where regularly you had to pass all the defendants waiting for their cases to be heard on the stairs. Many times we have said if we had not had Bradfield, which housed young tearaways from all over the country and if we took six or seven families out of the Tiverton and Cullompton area, we would have only needed two or three youth courts a year! Various training events were held and one of the best was the annual trip to Saunton Sands Hotel where we combined with the North Devon Benches in a most glorious setting. On these occasions I met a few ex-Young Farmers who had also joined the Bench. In 2000 we saw the amalgamation of many of the rural courts into the Central Devon Bench covering an area from the Dorset border to Okehampton. The closure of local courts was opposed by a few, as we were appointed mainly because of our local knowledge of the District. In the Central Devon Bench, with the merger of all the smaller Benches there are approximately one-hundred and fifty magistrates and again I met another set of colleagues of various occupations. At first it was a nervous start, as we had to adapt to their ways of running a court. What I did experience was a far greater variety of cases, many much more serious than we had previously seen at our local court. In Exeter there were many drug cases and serious assaults within the city. The Youth Court had a superb young offender's team who were very devoted to rehabilitating young offenders. Most of the Exeter and Wonford

Bench had their particular day to sit, and I being able to sit on any day meant I soon met lots of new colleagues. The constant changing of law meant more and more training days, with me feeling that the Government never lets anything settle to see the result of a law. Giving offenders caught red-handed CREDIT for a guilty plea sticks hard in the throat and the knowledge that a prisoner will only serve half the prison sentence is sometimes difficult to understand in our legal system. Now a sentence of less than 56 days will result in a defendant serving probably three days as well as being given a financial sum on release.

On the amalgamation of our Benches I was appointed to the Bench Training and Development Committee for three years. It was pointed out, that new chairmen needed more experience in this post, so after twelve years I gave up taking the chair to become a permanent winger. In my early days as a chairman, one could admonish and tell the defendants exactly how you felt, but then after new training we were told to say nothing but the sentence that was imposed. Chairmen now have to give reasons why defendants are found guilty or not, why we give them bail or not and that scourge of the modern day, form filling, gets worse. In 2003 the then chairman of the Lord Chancellor's Advisory Sub Committee Anne Davies (who walked our farm regularly), persuaded me to apply to join it, for she was sure I would find it interesting. After thought I applied and went through to an interview process, of which I am not too experienced. I was appointed to this committee in 2004 which included experienced magistrates and non magistrates. Each year, we interviewed candidates who must demonstrate they have six key qualities. They are good character, understanding and communication, social awareness, maturity and sound temperament, sound judgement, commitment and reliability – surprisingly common sense is not necessary! I found the interviewing a rewarding exercise, as we recommend names to the Lord Chancellor, those who we think after training would make good magistrates.

Some Memorable Cases

At Cullompton a defendant in the cells escaped through the roof, and we heard him run across the top of Court Two. On descent he was chased up the main street, but evaded recapture for several days!

One day I was thrust into the chair due to the unexplainable absence of a senior colleague, I and my newly appointed colleague magistrate were faced with a full court room of reporters and interested parties. The case was the first one brought in the country against a local vicar being ordered to repair or take down an unsafe church. Our Legal Advisor at the time advised us that the case should be adjourned but Mid Devon Council proceeded and I still have never been forgiven by locals of that church, for being instrumental in the order that was enforced. But the church was in very bad repair and even the vicar himself had received injuries from falling masonry, and there was a huge danger to people tending graves.

One case was of a well known television presenter who was appearing for having a fourth conviction for speeding in twelve months. This resulted in her being banned from driving for six months. In the witness box, she was not prepared to answer questions on her salary or her family. Furthermore we found no special reasons not to disqualify her for the obligatory six months. She came to court with no money other than an American Express Card, which failed to activate and had to be brought back to court and told payment would have to be made within fourteen days. We were told by the usher at the end of the morning session, after being banned from that moment on, she got into her car and drove from the Court House. Subsequently she made a written complaint against me and the Legal Advisor in the way that she was dealt with. After a thorough investigation by the Chief Justices Clerk, he found no grounds for her complaints.

I also remember a time when we sent a persistent offender to prison as well as ordering him to pay compensation to the victim. On leaving the dock with the security staff, he hurled a handful of coins at the bench with a comment "This is all you will get!"

At Exeter, I remember the case of an Oakford farmer, who was charged with careless driving. Whilst driving his tractor and hay turner along a quiet country road, he startled a horse rider who was flung off onto the road. She rang the police who pursued the farmer for two miles trying to attract his attention before he was stopped. At court I have never seen such a dirty, dishevelled farmer, who I am sure could be smelt coming from at least one-hundred yards! We were pre-warned of his appearance and all windows in the court room were fully opened, whilst his case was dealt with very swiftly. I learnt later that he worked and slept in the same clothes living in a farm house with no running water, only a stream.

A fine defaulter was brought to court owing a fine of £400, for failing to identify the driver of a vehicle. She was accompanied by a "Mackenzie friend" (not a qualified lawyer), to speak on her behalf. Firstly he insisted he wore his beret hat in court which was refused. He then demanded all the names of everyone in court – again refused. After removing an A4 leaflet from a suitcase he proceeded to talk "gibberish" for the next five minutes ending with "the fine will be paid by the Treasury and is sealed by a red finger print at the bottom of the page." Not one of us in court understood a word he said, but he was left in no doubt by the chairman that payment would be expected within the next fourteen days. We later learnt they were from a peculiar commune at Risdon near Okehampton.

Last Year as a Magistrate – 2009

I will never regret becoming a magistrate and hope I have given back something to the community in public service working as a team. Never would I have met so many colleagues of so many professions. It keeps your mind active and I have heard more excuses for committing a crime, than I have had hot dinners! It has been frustrating on many occasions, waiting for solicitors and advocates to be ready on time to present their case satisfactorily. Sometimes the police and the Crown Prosecution Service, fail to present their case satisfactorily. I also feel our hands are tied firmly behind our backs, in not being able to punish in the way we would like because of written law. As magistrates we know which advocates we would have represent us, if unfortunately we fell foul of the law. I remember a CPS prosecutor who would bend over backwards to help an unrepresented defendant, especially if he was repentant over his misdeeds. He did not suffer fools lightly and could be a hard prosecutor, not giving an inch. Did I enjoy being a magistrate? Enjoy, is the wrong word. How can you enjoy punishing your fellow man! There but for the Grace of God go I.

As I retire from being a Justice of the Peace. I can see there are going to be difficult times ahead. The continuing budget cuts to both the court and probation services give me cause for concern. Efficiency cuts yes, but there have been deep cuts over the last two years and before long the effects will show in the criminal justice system in both the operation and the public view of the service. "If you squeeze all the juice out of an orange, it does not eat well", likewise the Criminal Justice System. I worry, to some extent, about the future of the magistracy, with the use of more District Judges and the use of more police penalty notices for a further range of offences.

I and many other colleagues were amazed, at a recent Magistrates Association AGM, when a prison governor did not realise that we were part of the judicial system!! Now we have their association asking us not to sentence anyone to under twelve months custody. This would effectively

My colleagues on the Bench.

mean that we could not sentence anyone to custody in the magistrates court. Time and time again, I hear people say "they have given up reporting crime to the police," because of their lack of response. A recent survey quoted that only 4% of all crime reported reached a successful outcome. Local justice has disappeared to a degree with the closure of so many local courts. When I was appointed to the Bench, I sat in my area of local knowledge but now the Central Devon Bench stretches from the Dorset border to Dartmoor. I do hope that we give more "credit" to the victims of crime than to the defendant and that, despite all the dramatic changes, the magistrates will still have a vital role for many years to come.

I feel that without my YFC training in public speaking competitions, I would not have been able to sit, chair and discuss cases in the magistrates court. But it has led me to see a much wider side of life.

Belinda Dixon from Radio Devon.

Pippa Quelch recording with Farmer John.

CHAPTER EIGHT
FARMER JOHN ON
RADIO DEVON

Early in 1997 I received a call from John Govier of Radio Devon, to ask if I would come into the studio at Exeter, to talk about farming and conservation topics, after winning the Otter Trophy for Devon. The competition is organised by the farming wildlife advisory group yearly and awarded to the farm which has combined business and conservation to the best effect. Never having been interviewed on radio before, I felt rather nervous as this programme was going out "live" and not pre-recorded. The studio in Exeter is at St David's Hill and shares an entrance with a chiropractor practice, so I had to make sure I went to the right area! The recording rooms are downstairs, and the other JG met me and showed me to the studio and our respective seats. Headphones attached, we waited for the live start signal, and began talking about our work on the farm, and conservation objectives. It always seemed easy, to talk about something you enjoy, and I think it must have gone well for John asked me to come again in a month's time. I finished my contribution with "That's a proper job", which became my sign off words for the next eleven years. The first year the programme went out at mid day on a Monday. The next month's programme went well, and John decided I should become a regular contributor each month. The following month was different, as I was in the Exeter studio and JG in Plymouth. This was quite a different experience, as I was on my own in the Exeter studio speaking into a microphone. It was after this episode that I suggested JG (or the BBC) should buy himself a pair of wellies, and come out onto the farm, where he could fully understand the workings and sounds of the countryside.

At this time, we kept suckler cows and sheep, while also growing corn and roots for their consumption. Each month I tried to present our farming practices and talk about the issues affecting our industry, plus coming events in the local area. Safety issues were made clear, and I well remember one of John's visits when we went up to a field behind the farm house to meet the suckler herd. As we went up the steep entrance to the field I sent my dog in, as I for one know the dangers of cows with young calves when a dog is present. This was John's first lesson of walking in the countryside. Lying under an old oak tree, was my very quiet Charolais bull (Bimbo). As we approached John's anxiety was clear to see. So I reassured him he would be safe, if he could run one-hundred yards in under ten seconds – Bimbo usually took 10.5! John visited at lambing, hay making and corn harvesting times, and people seemed to enjoy our rambles. But after twelve months I was given a new presenter, a sweet young lady, Belinda Dixon, who would probably be the first to acknowledge she was a city girl with much to learn about the countryside. We were probably a good match, as an educational presentation at 7.40 on a Saturday morning needed to be bright and cheerful. Her first visit in May was while I was turning hay with a tractor, and haybob in a field close to the farm buildings. Belinda's first question was "How many acres are you cutting today?" I then knew it would take some time, to educate her into my farming ways and traditions.

After twelve months working with Belinda and our continuing development of tree planting and pond creation, we decided to have a public walk in April annually to see both the farm, and a beautiful bluebell walk in some of our ancient woodland. We were winners of the Farming and Wildlife Advisory Group Devon Woodland Flower Competition. We did not charge for this experience but have asked for donations to various charities over the years. Some we have supported include the MS society, Leukaemia Research and latterly Children's Hospice South West. Radio Devon set out to raise a million pounds in its Chestnut Appeal, which was for specialist treatment for prostate cancer patients here in Devon. In August that year, we did two walks which raised nearly £2000 for their charity – phew wasn't it hot! It was actually the hottest

Pippa Quelch from Radio Devon.

ountry Courier

'Farmer John' hosts a guided walk

TREES, wildlife, ponds and nature were placed under the spotlight when BBC Radio Devon's own "Farmer John" hosted a guided walk at Way Farm, Thorverton.

About 70 people attended the event organised by Devon Farming and Wildlife Advisory Group (FWAG) with farming advisory service, ADAS.

John Greenslade (62), was born at Way Farm, Thorverton, near Bickleigh Castle, and has lived there all his life.

His grandfather came to the farm in 1916 as a tenant under the Fursdon Estate.

The family purchased the farm from the estate in the early 50's and in 1973 added a further five large river meadows adjacent to the River Exe, which now runs along the eastern boundary of the farm.

Way Farm is a total of 168 acres which varies from gradual to very steep slopes consisting of grassland, woodland and four nature areas.

John and his wife Janette

ran, primarily, a dairy farm until 1987. Today it is stocked with a suckler beef herd and sheep.

About 10 years ago, when Devon County Council were giving away 25 free trees to any land owner who would have them, John became interested in planting more.

In the last nine years John has planted between 60 and 70 acres of hardwood trees and completed a massive farm trail.

John is now paid to plant trees and receives a yearly grant to take the farm out of production, particularly corn production.

Ponds have been created and the farm now boast five wildlife, including otters and Kingfishers.

Three years ago he started broadcasting regularly on BBC Radio Devon as 'Farmer John' and uses this to talk about life on the farm and about issues affecting farmers.

In 1996 John and Janette were joint winners of the Devon Bronze Otter Award for Farm Conservation in 1996 and Devon winners of the Woodland Wild Flower Competition in 1999.

At the Devon FWAG and ADAS day several speakers were on hand to contribute to the event. They focussed on

woodland planting and pond construction, game and wildlife.

John, who is also a local magistrate, said he opened up his farm to show the public how subsidies and grants were spent.

School groups have visited the farm as part of their studies in the past.

The general public is wel

come to visit the farm to walk the farm trail by prior arrangement only.

Telephone John or Janette on 01884 855354 to arrange an appointment.

Don't forget to wear suitable footwear and clothing.
alan-quick@crediton
couriernewspaper.co.uk

John and Janette Greenslade at Way Farm, Thorverton.

Advertising our walks at Way Farm.

Bluebell Walk for Children's Hospice South West 2009.

day of the year and we had iced drinks at the bottom of Woodwalls lane, but one dear old lady collapsed with heat exhaustion. Luckily there was a retired doctor on the walk who gave good advice, and Richard (son-in-law), rescued her with the bike and trailer. We continued to record even through the Foot and Mouth, when no visits to the farm were allowed. We met in various locations, when I could let go my frustrations at the inadequate handling by those in charge – then MAFF. Nothing was learnt from previous outbreaks and their immediate action was lamentable. It was important for those of us who were lucky enough to not be infected to support those whose only contact with the outside world was with telephone and radio. We were recording once, outside St David's church in Exeter when half way through the church bells rang out, and believe it or not, complaints came from listeners about the background noise. Belinda planted a white elm in an area of the farm; here we had lost all our English elm trees due to disease. This was the first tree planted in a 14 acre field, and hopefully is resistant to Dutch elm disease. Also during these years working with Belinda, I discussed extracts from a book on "Grandmothers Cures", for various ailments, which led to many humorous listener comments. Many others sent in their individual cures on post cards. Every Devon County Show we recorded the May programme from the show ground, and during this time we started a competition for each month. Some were identifying bird songs, sounds of the countryside and noises from the countryside. Sadly these competitions were stopped, when the national competition scandal was revealed. It was a shame, for we got quite a mail bag where we received useful contributions from the listeners. One competition was to identify what DEFRA stands for, and the best I found was from a Mrs Johnson from Seaton, whose answer was the Department for the Eradication of Farming and Rural Affairs!

May 2007, saw me working with a new presenter. With Pippa Quelch like most women, a sense of direction is something lacking, and she found difficulty in finding our "out in the sticks" farm. Eventually finding us, I was ready with quad bike and trailer, to show her around the farm. Pippa is a lovely girl, professional, easy to work with and having a wicked sense of humour. She recorded more than was needed, but edited it well. Her sense of humour was obvious from day one. As we were about to set off up over the farm, I had accidently left the stop button on the quad and it took some time for me to start. Little did I know she had recorded this episode and had kept it in her first presentation. Listeners gave me good advice as to where I could get the bike started! Seeking some sort of revenge, a couple of months later, we were recorded close to one of our ponds, when after a while she enquired if the "two ducks on the pond were ok?" My reply was sadly their "legs were tied to the bottom of the pond." After a frowning expression she realised they were plastic but very realistic – revenge is sweet!

As we were, at this time, cutting down on our livestock on the farm, we monthly paid several visits to neighbouring farms to give a true reflection of how varied the farming industry is. We paid a visit to my son-in-law's farm at Kentisbeare where the local vet was doing a herd health visit. At Richards's father's dairy cow sale, where the cows were being sold in guineas, I was surprised that she did not know the value of a guinea. I remember at a Devon County Show recording the judging of Saddleback pigs, one sow came over and laid right in front of Pippa. She was worried if it was ok. I was able to assure her that the pig was only sulking for she had not won a prize. Another experience of recording a monthly programme was when I was in hospital prior to a kidney stone operation. Pippa recorded the programme from my hospital bed! As Pippa developed her programme she began to introduce our monthly chats with very appropriate music. On the twenty fifth anniversary of Radio Devon she planted an oak and two spindle trees in our new piece of woodland. The oak tree was grown from an acorn in our garden, and was the first tree to be planted in February 2008. In the centre of the field we included another pond, with its complement of plastic ducks!

What has been amusing about this experience is the numerous times that I have been identified by my voice, "Devonshire Brogue", sometimes in hospital or meeting people at shows and other various events. After eleven years of Farmer John the BBC felt in its wisdom that Radio Devon had had enough of my rambles, and changed the content of Pippa's programme. It was perhaps disappointing that it took three weeks into the new programmes before I was told that my services were no longer required, by the new producer. It would have been nice, to close my contributions with a final programme, where I could have thanked all my neighbours and friends, who had helped to make Farmers John's contribution "a proper job". In some way, though, this feeling of not completing a final programme has given me the inspiration to write this book and give it the title. Thanks Radio Devon, for giving me the opportunity to present the countryside to one and all, each month.

With Princess Anne at Devon County Show shearing competitions.

Opposite: *Mid Devon Show Officials.*

CHAPTER NINE
MID DEVON SHOW, SHEARING COMPETITIONS, PLOUGHING MATCHES AND THE SILVANUS TRUST

Mid Devon Show

It is said, that from little acorns come big trees. Well, after the demise of the old Tiverton Show and the Town and Country Show in 1971, Roger Hill had on many occasions put the thought to me of bringing back an agricultural one day show with a difference. The Mid Devon area had a gap in late July to fit this event into. Roger was a Trustee of the Tiverton Agriculture Association to which, through the generosity of the Amory family, money was given from the sale of the old show field in 1974. The interest from the money, which was invested, was to be used to help finance agriculture, horticulture, silviculture and Young Farmers Clubs, which were within a thirteen mile radius of Tiverton Town Hall. Roger

HOPING to bridge the gap between town and country: (Left to right) show secretary Marilyn Daw; treasurer Tony Sloley; chairman Roger Hill; vice chairman and show director, John Greenslade; and show host, Geoffrey Clapp.

took this idea to the committee and with Tom Penny's (secretary of the Trustees) help, a meeting was called on the 26th of June 1991, inviting many local farmers, business men and others for their views and help. At this meeting a site subcommittee was set up, and sites for the show suggested were at Chettiscombe,

Show chief is man with a mission

A FARMER with a mission to cultivate new ties of friendship between town and country is Bickleigh's John Greenslade.

Mr Greenslade is founding director of the new Mid Devon Show, which is to be held next year.

He said: "I believe in bringing town and country together, and I hope that the show will make a major contribution to that.

"It amazes me that even in a rural county like Devon so many children — and grown-

BICKLEIGH

ups too — know so little about life on the farm."

Mr Greenslade farms 160 acres with his wife Janette.

He is already practising what he preaches by fostering visits to his farm by schoolchildren, including pupils of his local village school at Bickleigh.

With help from Devon County Council

he is creating new walks on his farm to open it up for organised visits in the summer.

He believes the new show on Geoff Clapp's Hartnoll Farm, Tiverton, will help to bring town and country folk together.

"A lot of us felt that a big gap was left when the Tiverton Show ended in 1970," he said. "We believe that this new event will plug that gap."

The show will be held on July 28, 1994.

John Greenslade

Mid Devon Show.

Hartnoll Farm and a site at Junction 27 of the M5 at Sampford Peverell. We were looking for a site of sixty to seventy acres; advice was sought from Mid Devon District Council for planning permission, police for road access, sponsorship, programmes, a secretary and advice on all legal requirements.

Many meetings later, a date of Thursday the 29th of July was proposed for the first show and in 1994 at Hartnoll Farm. This date was later adjusted to Saturday the 23rd of July. At a meeting on the 8th of December 1993 officers were elected with Roger Hill as Chairman, myself as Show Director, Treasurer Tony Sloley and Secretary Marilyn Daw taking over from Tom Penny from the 1st of January 1993. The first president was to be Sir John Palmer, a solicitor from a local firm. Prior to the first show, much help was given by the North Devon and Honiton Shows in Mid Devon's preparations. Our show was somewhat different to others, by having working demonstrations in adjoining fields. There were sheep dog demonstrations with the usual main ring attractions, livestock and poultry competitions and many varied trade stands. The Tiverton group of YFCs was to hold its rally on the site and heavy horses and vintage machinery sections were proposed.

We were only able to put this show on the road, because of the huge offers of sponsorship, trophies, and the tremendous work of many stewards before and after the show. Remember we started with little financial backing, other than a £10,000 loan from the Tiverton Agriculture Association. We were certainly in the hands of the weather for the first show; many sections of the show had meetings prior to the first show, with the aim to give visitors good value, good entertainment, good education, with good easy traffic entry and exit. Show day brought ideal weather and the public gave us great support, with estimated visitors of 12 to 14,000 which exceeded all expectations. All this support, led to a £16,000 profit on the show, allowing us to transfer £10,000, into a "Rainy Day Fund". Many lessons were learnt about running a successful one day show, including health and safety regulations, and keeping all roads to and from the show moving. But the great success of Mid Devon Show was achieved by the enthusiasm and working together of the voluntary stewards which made the show tick.

The following shows were equally as successful, marred only by a freak accident to a young girl, which sadly made the headlines. After three years, we three main officers – Chairman, Secretary and Show Director – decided to hand over our offices to a new committee. The success of the show was giving others ideas with which the show could go forward. I was not happy with some of these ideas, so a new show committee with a full time paid secretary was formed, but I still remained a firm supporter of the Mid Devon Show. Several years later, I came back into office as the Trade Stand Chairman, and enjoyed working with Captain Dereck Thomas, as Show Director. During this time, I was experiencing severe kidney stone problems, and was unable to fully commit myself to the show, which eventually in 2007 led me to resign my position. In 2001 the outbreak of Foot and Mouth disease led to its cancellation, as was the case with many other one day shows. In 2007, after a terribly wet summer, a decision was taken that the ground was not fit to hold the July show. Many other one day shows were cancelled. This was a very difficult decision, and a costly exercise, but I believe it would have been a mud bath for visitors to the show. 2008 was again a wet summer but Mid Devon was blessed with a dry period and held a very successful show. The 2009 show experienced a very wet July and it was debateable whether the show could go ahead. The weather forecasters predicted a dry show day, and the show went ahead with a good attendance. The show field held up well, but clearing up in the following week was a muddy messy job. The VIP marquee boss said the show should be renamed "The Mud Devon Show!"

It gives me great pride, that those discussions in the early 1990s with Roger Hill, led to the Mid Devon show being regarded as one of the best in the West Country. In retains its objectives of being a truly country, family and friendly show giving the general public an insight into everything good on our farms, and in the countryside.

Shearing Competitions

Over our family's farming life, we have always kept sheep, and one of the necessities of sheep farming is that they have to be shorn annually. I learnt to shear at Withleigh Young Farmers annual shearing classes, held on local farms. We were taught, to make a good and clean job, without cutting the skin of the sheep. Our instructors were Jack Hamett and Clive Hopper, who taught us to use both left and right hands while clipping the sheep. There was also the skill of tying up the fleeces in a tidy fashion to present it the Wool Marketing Board. Although I did not win many competitions at YFC (I think as I was tall, I got backache much too often!) I was always a keen supporter of seeing a job well done. The early competitions at Devon County Show, were only for YFC members with just three judges, one being my good friend Albert Cook.

In the 1970s Clive Hopper was the senior steward at these show competitions, when he asked me to become a steward prior the show. I was asked to help add up the scores and produce the results for the final presentation. During this time, I met many other helpers, who like me have retained their admiration for shearing competitions and many of them are still involved today. One stalwart, was dear old Jack Coker who kept the

Noel Edmonds presenting awards at the Devon County Show.

World Shearing Championship at Bath and West Show.

wool and boards tidy all the time. And in later years we presented him with a wide broom to make his job easier. He was a cheery chap to work with, full of inspiration, especially to new beginners. His son Roy became a first class shearer, winning many competitions representing England as a competitor and a judge. Whilst the Devon County was held at the old Whipton show ground, the Bowen shearing method came which made shearing a much easier and faster job. The old Whipton show ground had a reputation of getting very muddy in the middle of May, and I remember many years of struggling in the marquee to keep the sheep and wool dry.

In the early 1980s I took on as the senior steward, and was privileged in leading a first class team, that in 1984 which won the Wilkinson Sword – presented by Noel Edmonds for initiative and team work. In 1983, my daughter Sally was the reserve sheep shearing champion at Withleigh YFC finals, and she competed at Devon County Show. In 1985, I again was privileged to show and introduce stewards and competitors alike to our then President Princess Anne, who showed much interest in our section. Through shearing competitions I was privileged to meet some of the best shearers around the world who competed at the Devon show. Shearers came, from New Zealand, Australia, England, Wales, Scotland, Norway, and other countries, and we met them most years, taking in part in the competitions. Around this time, I was invited by Cornwall YFC County Organiser, Mick Allsey to do the scoring at the Royal Cornwall Show. I have continued to work at the show ground ever since but in later years, with "computer whizz kid" Arther Rundle. Arther's early computer model did not like damp conditions, but its use was far less taxing on the brain cells. In one difficult wet year, when we were calculating manually, our late good friend Wesley Wilton, was overlooking and his comment "have you divided by two?" was quickly enacted by Arther and me. We regularly laugh about it, and exchange Christmas cards, which are signed with the ÷2! Wesley was a stalwart of the World Golden Shears Competitions. In 1992, these competitions were held at the Bath and West show ground, Shepton Mallet. I was invited to be a liaison officer to get competitors from the competing countries to and fro by bus from their accommodation at a holiday camp at the North Coast. Shearers do seem to consume plenty of beer, and it was a difficult job to raise them up in the morning in time for competitions. Again this gave me the opportunity to meet competitors and judges from all over the world including Godfrey Bowen.

During the last few years Arther Rundle has been the Chief Steward at the Bath and West shearing stand, and I have assisted with the scoring there. Two of these years, are memorable for the torrential rain, which flooded the pens and seating area of the shed. Arther is now the secretary, of the National Golden Shears World Council, and as such was involved in the 2008 finals in Norway. We, at the last minute, decided to go and support the English teams, which included George and Andrew Mudge from Tavistock in Devon. They were the first father and son to compete at world finals. In the Team Hand Clipping, they came an incredible fourth, and George was sixth in the individual final. The Norwegians were first class hosts, spending more than a million pounds on the finals, which I understand was fully sponsored. We stayed with a family in the local village south of Stavanger. They were typically friendly Norwegians who spoke very good English. During the trip, we went to the welcoming ceremony, which was held in a cave underground which seated 350 people. We also went on a fjord trip, and visited and viewed some very steep sheep and fruit farms. In Norway sheep are housed in the winter and after spring lambing, go up into the mountains until October when they are then brought home to base, where the lambs and ewes are shorn; lambs then go the abattoir. This trip was made possible because of my connections with shearing competitions and the friendship forged between me and judges, competitors and stewards alike. In 2010, the World Golden Shears will be held at the Royal Welsh show ground, Builth Wells.

Ploughing Matches and the Tiverton Agriculture Association
Ploughing competitions have been running in Devon for more than a hundred years, especially the Cruwys Morchard and Withleigh as well as the Witheridge and district. These competitions are a countryside tradition, which needs to be kept going as long as possible. The competitors show great pride in making a first class job, and even today we still have horse ploughing competitions, ploughing with vintage tractors and modern tractors. They are judged on the way they start, turn the furrows and finish, their plots. The first recorded match at Witheridge took place in 1840, which included classes for servants of agriculture who had worked for the same master for the longest time and the best testimonials. As years went by, classes for roots, hedging, thatching, rope and spar making became regular features. It was not until 1937 that tractor ploughing competitions were introduced. We can still see old Standard Fordsons and Ransome ploughs at all matches today. Many local ploughmen represented their area in national competitions; they include Jack Nott and Raymond

My brother-in-law at a ploughing match.

Govier who have won national recognition. In 2005, I took Radio Devon's Pippa Quelch to record her programme there, when I was asked to judge, the roots, hay, silage and corn classes. Whilst at the Cruwys match last year, I was approached by Sir Ian Amory who asked me to consider whether I would take on the chair of the Tiverton Agriculture Association Trustees. I had been a Trustee for several years, which Sir Ian had chaired very professionally with a touch of "Amory Humour". The Trustees meet twice a year, to decide upon the distribution of the interest from investments to honourable people, and organisations within the area. We have helped to finance YFC exchange visits, ploughing matches, flower and vegetable shows and other worthwhile projects, of which the Mid Devon show was one. Again I felt honoured to be asked to take on the chair, from such a well respected gentlemen, and he was duly made the Life President of our charity.

At the present time we are supporting local schools, in helping them produce their own vegetables for the school kitchens. This gives school children a hands-on experience of where the food on their table comes from. Tiverton will always be grateful to the Amory family for their foresight in giving back something that will help to maintain countryside education, and events in the locality. In latter years, I have been asked to judge, grass, hay, roots and corn at local ploughing matches, which is certainly interesting in visiting a number of farms in the local district. At

Cullompton, we have been taken around by local farmer, "Tex" Tidball who is a countryside character, giving good humorous commentary as we travel around visiting the various crops, and then the static exhibits on show day.

The Silvanus Trust

The Silvanus Trust began in 1983, as part of the Dartington Action Research Trust, which was responding to worries about the neglect of broadleaf woodlands. It was conceived as an integrated rural development project, linking all these constituent parts of the woodland process. Primary goals were to conserve woodland habitats, develop rural employment in forestry and related industries, and also to develop timber markets to increase the economic value of woodlands. The trust has delivered this mission for over 25 years, increasing widely across the South West region and in the process has supported, communities, schools, businesses and individuals creating and sustaining woodlands, partnerships and jobs. The trust aims to inspire and involve communities to manage and value trees and woodland. We do this through education, training, and community projects.

Our Woodland Renaissance Project is a large scale partnership which will have an impact upon the forestry sector across the region. Through this partnership grants can be given to any work in woodlands or with timber, which will have strategic economic impact across the South West. I became involved as a trustee of this charity after using the commercial arm of this charity Silvanus Services Ltd. They had been involved in the planning and planting of my woodland, since 1995, although most of their work had been in Cornwall and South Devon. So I was invited to become a trustee in 2000 to widen the area that they operated in, and in view of my interest in planting more broadleaf woodlands. Our Chairman is Sir Robert Hicks, a retired MP from North Cornwall and the rest of the trustees, are all well respected foresters. At the time of me joining, our offices were in Launceston and later moved to Stoke Climsland with an extra office for two years at Bradninch. We had a director and six staff, and relied on grants and European funding for many of our projects. In the early days, this funding was much more freely available than it is today – a smaller pot of money and more organisations applying for it.

After three years it was a bit of a surprise, that we had a management buyout proposal, from Silvanus Services Ltd. It was not a unanimous decision of the trustees to sell but it had become obvious it was difficult to

retain any ambitious managers for any period of time. After the sale, we began negotiations to buy and revitalize a Cornish sawmill at Lostwithiel. After getting all grants and finance in place (taking nearly two years), and a good number of timber growers supporting the project, a last minute change of bank personnel altered their minds about the funding. We could not continue with this project, but some of our supporters gave the owner enough encouragement to stay with the business. The whole exercise cost the trust a great deal of money and time spent, which was not compensated for. Our then director resigned to start her own wool business, and we appointed an excellent replacement, the only disadvantage was that she knew only a little about the woodland industry. Most of her time in recent years, has been seeking out new projects, where funding from Europe and national governments could assist, but with the credit crisis deepening and less money available many similar charities are fighting for that pot of money. As a charity that relies on this funding, like many others, times are difficult and we have been looking to other charitable organisations with similar objectives to join with. Our biggest coup was that Woodland Renaissance which we have run, with Jez Ralph at the head for a few years, has had its contract renewed for a further period.

We continually hear credits about the work of the trust, which is highly respected in the industry. We hope we can find our way through this difficult period, working from a new office at Trematon, Saltash in Cornwall. I am so impressed with the quality of the employees, that I invited the trust to take on the management of Byway Woodlands, and an agreement was drawn up which both sides wish to see go ahead. To date, this has been held from ongoing because of the financial position of the trust and some doubt about its future. Byway Woodlands would have been a base for new and old woodland training and education. We await the future of this project with hope that it can go ahead. Again I have been extremely fortunate to meet such an experienced group of trustees, using their expertise within their individual sections of the woodland industry.

Our very first pond.

Bluebells in spring.

CHAPTER TEN
TREES, PONDS, WILDFLOWERS AND WILDLIFE

I suppose we have always had an interest in trees and conservation. In the 1980s when Devon County Council had some spare money, people with land were offered up to twenty five trees to plant in appropriate places. We took up this offer for three or four years, planting up in corners of fields and adjoining pieces of woodland. From time to time, the Devon County Forester came and inspected and made sure they were well cared for. In 1994 we started serious planting of trees, starting with some of the steeper land. We took advice from Jackie Scott, who was our local Devon FWAG advisor; we looked at what trees grew well on our land already and made these our main types of tree in our plan. Glades and paths were also put into the plan, so we could easily link up a farm trail. In our first planting we planted oak, ash, wild cherry, lime, chestnut, with small groups of maple, crab apple, mountain ash and for the edge of our rides we used hazel, blackthorn, Guelder rose, honeysuckle with wayfarer and spindle. These varieties would create a lot of food for the birds in late summer and winter. It was decided to plant in wavy lines, but with groups of fifteen to twenty of each variety. The initial reaction of neighbours and Bickleigh village that overlooked across the valley was that they did not like the "statues" of green guards which were necessary to protect the trees from roe deer and rabbits. These guards also provided a greenhouse effect, giving quicker growth to the saplings. Although not a big user of sprays, it was necessary to kill the competing grass and weeds around a metre of each tree, for the first two years. I bought a mini-tractor with topper to trim between trees and clear the paths.

The following year, we did another three sites, containing the same species but adding groups of Scotch pine, silver birch, walnut a few beech and some aspen, with further glades and footpaths. Help to fund these schemes came from the farm woodland premium scheme from which we receive annual payments for fifteen years. DEFRA regularly inspected to see they were being cared for. In 1996 after being encouraged to enter the Devon Bronze Otter Award for farm conservation, we came joint first, and in 1999 we won the Devon woodland wildflower competition. With the prize money of £500, we took advice from friend and expert Cyrl Cole about the construction of a pond in Way Moor. We knew this area was well clay based, and it took two days to construct. We were given wetland plants to put around the edge of the pond, these being yellow flag, bull rush, blue iris, pickerel weed, purple loosestrife, marsh marigold and water plantain. In an amazingly short time these plants established, and frogs, toads, dragonflies and damselflies came to use the facilities. Our friendly vet Alan Hopkins gave us some tench and rudd. Soon we had visits from wild ducks and kingfishers, and the occasional Canada geese in winter. In the new woodland we soon began to see wild flowers evolve that I remember seeing as a child, devils bit, scabious, red campions, cuckoo flowers, great mullein, stitchwort, mallow, knapweed, toadflax, fleabane and many others which we have recorded. Our interest in pond creation has been recognised by FWAG who have held pond seminars at the farm on several occasions. We can show prospective pond builders different ages of when our ponds were built, and can follow how they have developed over the years.

Each year, something new appears and more and more orchids in the pasture land. We have planted *wild* daffodils in our small area of ancient woodland which is blessed with a carpet of bluebells in April; twenty-six varieties of woodland flowers were also found in this wood alone. On the edge of Five Journeys I planted a long row of buddleia on the south facing side of the wood. Each year, they have a huge array of flowers and in a decent summer, attract hordes of butterflies. As yet we have not kept a note of the different types of butterfly, but an expert who lives in Bickleigh village has been quite impressed with numerous varieties on show.

We have been involved in the RSPB farm bird count in 2003, when thirty different birds were seen on two visits. We could add another five to that list which we see regularly. In 2004 after having seven or eight barn owl boxes in various sheds, we were elated to find young barn owls in one of the barns. Our friend and vet Alan Hopkins got permission to film them with infra-red cameras, which showed the night comings and goings over the next month. It was a brilliant film showing the adult owls feeding their young at night. Another experience is to dissect an owl pellet which gives an indication of what mammals they are feeding on. Over 2009 we have seen them breeding again in the same shed, with the hope of another sitting in another shed. Over the years, other bird boxes have been erected, regularly used by tits, sparrows

Left: *Receiving the Woodland Award.*

Middle left: *Receiving Otter Award from FWAG.*

Lower left: *Receiving Woodland Award at Devon County Show.*

Below: *Oliver the owl.*

and other woodland birds. We see green and spotted woodpeckers in our garden. Two years ago, we were advised that we had dormice on the farm, and we erected a dozen boxes. This spring we found three occupied by dormice, and others being used as blue tit nests. In our garage swallows come back and nest each year, but sadly no house martins. Having the River Exe bordering our eastern boundary, we have in the last year or two seen dippers, kingfishers, little egrets, swans, herons, goosanders and moorhens. Over the years we have planted many more acres of trees, and built seven ponds.

Those who were disturbed by our statues will now tell you in the spring and autumn the colours of the trees blend well into the country side. Now semi-retired we derive much pleasure from watching through our bungalow kitchen window, the huge number of wild birds at our feeders. I told Jan I shall have to start growing peanuts! At the bottom of our last planting we have left our mark, by planting our names in a short beech hedge.

There seems to be a continuing threat to our industry, whether it be livestock, or woodland. First has been the Foot and Mouth outbreaks, one outbreak from DEFRA's own laboratories, BSE which hit the beef market hard for some years, Avian Flu a threat to the poultry industry which is brought from the continent by migrating birds, and now there are various strains of Blue Tongue, which means that farmers have to vaccinate their animals annually. Others in the background, are Swine Fever in pigs, and African Horse Sickness. In woodland Sudden Oak Death affects oak trees of fifty plus years. Also Phytophthora Ramorum which is affecting Rhododendrons, a Bleeding Stem Canker which can be passed on to other trees. I suppose we always have to fight disease in the agriculture industry – it is part of the job!

Over the last few years, I have been written nature notes, on a monthly basis, for the "Bickleigh Bugle" magazine relating the sights, sounds, and nature's wonders here at the farm. I have tried to illustrate, especially for those who are not able to come and see for themselves, what a lovely countryside we have here in the Exe Valley. I also give our monthly rainfall total, which certainly exceeded our yearly average over the last three years: is this global warming I ask? I have also made monthly contributions on farming matters, to the "Silverleigh Parish Newsletter" which covers the villages of Silverton, Butterleigh, Bickleigh, and Cadeleigh. I write under the title of "Farmer John's Rambles" relating to the relevant issues of the farming world as I see them. I am not actively involved in livestock, arable or grass farming, but I do care for the future of the industry.

We hope that others will over the years, be able to enjoy the pleasures of our farm and the countryside around.

The Three S's of Farmers' Weather Forecasting
Sounds Sights and Sayings

Living at Way Farm all my life we have learnt to listen and see signs of weather.

Sounds:
- If we can hear the mainline trains at Stoke Canon, rain is not far away.
- If we can hear the green woodpecker shouting (father always called it the wet wet bird), rain is not far away.
- If we can hear the River Exe it is said, that it is crying for more rain.

Sights:
- Swallows flying close to the ground, is not a good sign of sunny weather, likewise if flying high in the sky, it's good weather.
- In the morning, if you see cobwebs all over your lawn, across paths and in trees, it is a sign of good settled weather is to come.
- If the skylark (sadly not seen as often here) is high in the sky – good weather, if close to the ground – rain.
- If the sun is "drawing water", this is not as good sign for long fine weather.
- If the seagulls are "basket making", another sign of rain.
- Rings around the moon, not a good sign.
- If the long distant countryside looks very close, sign of rain.
- When cattle charge round with their tails in the air, thunder around.
- If rooks nest high in the trees, sign of a good summer.
- If the wind turns the backs of leaves to be showing, sign of showers.
- Put a Fur Cone on the window ledge, if it opens then dry weather is around, if closed rain is near.

Sayings
- If sheep go to shade in May, you will make very little good hay.
- Red sky at night, Shepherd's delight.
- Red sky in the morning, Shepherd's warning.
- The weather usually changes, with the new moon.
- East wind blowing in the winter brings snow.
- Oak leaves out before ash, a splash for summer.
- Ash before oak, a soak for the summer.
- 13 new moons in a year, does not bode good summer weather.
- Rain before 7 usually stops before 11.
- Ice in November to hold up a duck, the rest of the winter will be slush and muck.

Farmers usually keep an eye on the barometer, or hang up some seaweed outside the backdoor!

Wild Flowers on Way Farm

DRY

A Agrimony
Angelica

B Bird's Foot Trefoil
Bluebell
Buttercup
Broom
Burdock
Bindweed
Betony

C Celadine
Cranesbill
Charlock
Champion (White & Red)
Cow Parsley
Cuckoo Flower
Corn Cockle
Corn Flower
Colts Foot
Common Centaury
Cloves (Red & White)

D Dog Rose
Devils Bit Scabious
Dandelion
Daisy
Dead Nettle
Daffodil (Wild)

E Eyebright

F Flax
Foxglove
Fat Hen
Forget Me Not
Flea Bane
Field Gentian

G Gorse
Golden Rod
Greater Willow Herb
Garlic Mustard
Greater Plantain
Goats Beard

H Hogsweed
Hedge Mustard
Hedge Bindweed
Hawks Bit
Honey Suckle
Hemp Nettle

I Ivy

K Knap Weed

L Lords and Ladies
Ladies Bedstraw

M Mullien Great
Musk Mallow & Common
May Weed
Milk Maid

N Navel Wort
Nipple Wort

O Ox-Eye Daisy
Orchid Common
Spotted
Orchid Early Purple

P Penny Wort
Periwinkle
Pignut

Primrose
Poppy
Pansy (Wild)

R Ramsons
Rosebay Willow Herb
Red Shank
Ribwort
Reedmace

S Scarlet Pimpernel
Speedwell
Shepherds Purse
St John's Wort
Stitch Wort (Greater &
Lesser)
Strawberry (Wild)
Salad Burnet
Star of Bethlehem
Self Heal
Spurge
Solomon's Seal
Spear Thistle

T Three Cornered Leek
Toadflax

V Vetch (Corner & Tufted)
Valerian
Violet

W Wood Spurge
Wood Anemone
Wound Wort

Y Yarrow
Yellow Rattle
Yellow Archangel

WET

A Arrow Head

B Bistort
Bog Bean
Broomklime
Bulrush
Bedstraw

C Cuckoo Flower

F Fritillary Snakehead

I Indian Balsam

L Lesser Spearwort
Loosetrife (Purple & Yellow)

M Meadow Sweet
Marsh Marigold

O Orchid Heath Spotted

P Pickerell Weed

R Ragged Robin
Reedmace

W Water Violet
Water Forget Me Not
Water Plantain
Water Lily (Yellow & White)
Watercress
Water Mint
Water Crowfoot
Water Soldier
Wood Anemone

Y Yellow Iris Flag

My Poetic Sister Margaret.

CHAPTER ELEVEN
BITS AND PIECES
OF FUN AND LIFE

The Farmer's Lament

When I took up farming I was just a lad,
I looked at our pastures and my heart was glad,
I was ready to take on the world if need be,
And a good fruitful future was all I could see.

Then a man from the ministry came to my door,
and said, "Now young fellow you must produce more,
In London we've worked out a wonderful plan,
To double your output, make you a rich man".

"Half your land is just hedge and wood,
How can that possibly be any good?
Improve your acres and efficiency,
And I will make sure that you're paid handsomely."

So I followed his schemes, although it was hard,
When the last of the horses went from our yard,
I brought a new tractor and a big Ransomes plough;
It brings me to tears when I think of it now.
We ploughed up the scrubland, orchids and all,
And with great satisfaction watched the trees fall,
We burnt up the branches and blew out the stumps,
The ponds in the meadow were our rubbish dumps,

We grubbed out the hedges to make larger fields,
The bigger the better to increase our yields;

We worked on like beavers and never once paused,
And were paid very well for the havoc we caused.

Forty years on there's a knock at the door,
The man from the ministry, same as before;
"There's cash to made now if you plant a tree,
It's awfully exciting, I think you'll agree".

"We'd rather like some of your farm grow wild,
Just like you remember when you were a child;
A hedge by the hillside, a copse just beyond,
For fishes and frogs a nice stream and pond".

Well, now I'm newly retired and I sing this sad song,
Some of the things that I did were so wrong;
"What did the most damage?" I ask constantly,
"The man from the ministry, Dutch elm or me?"

Farmer John's Lament

Dairy Farmer's Lament

I long for a cow of modern make.
That milks five days for leisure's sake,
That sleeps on Saturdays, snores on
    Sundays
And starts afresh again on Mondays.

I long for a herd that knows the way
To wash each other day by day.
That never bothers to excite us.
With chills or fevers or mastitis.

I hope for a new and better breed
That takes less grooming and less feed,

That has the reason, wit and wisdom,
To use the seat and the flushing system.

I pray each week-end long and clear
Less work to do from year to year,
And cows that reach, production peak,
All in a five-day working week.

I long for officials, by the mob
To guide the farmers at their job,
and show those stupid breeders how
To propagate a five-day cow.

104

Silence of the Lambs

As the seasons roll relentlessly on
And from Winter emerges Spring
In the glorious Devonshire countryside
We will expect it to bring
Woodlands filled with birdsong
Hedgerows to break into bud
Cows in luxuriant meadows
Contentedly chewing their cud
Frisky Lambs bleat for their mothers
Each has its own special smell
It never ceases to amaze me
How from hundreds, theirs they can tell

But this Spring the country's in crisis
A deadly virus appeared
And from the green fields of Devon
The animals all have been cleared
The silence unnatural and eerie
Only the sounds of a bird
And from the usual noisy sheep and lambs
Not a sound is heard
The animals all have been slaughtered
And then buried or burnt
At least, let's hope when it's over
Some valuable lessons are learnt

Margaret Leach

My Dad was a Farmer

My Dad was a farmer, a man of the soil,
A life that he loved, despite blood, sweat and toil.
He'd plough the earth and sow the seeds,
Fertilize them and kill the weeds.
Then God would take over with enough rain and sun
To ripen the corn in the ears, every one,
The harvest was gathered and stored in the shed
For hungry animals in winter to be fed.

As the seasons rolled, with snow hail and rain,
The cycle of ploughing and tiling started over again
Dad milked the cows, he knew each one's name,
Today they're just numbers (I think that's a shame),
When lambs were born on a cold winter's night,
He'd get up and feed them, for each night he'd fight
'Twas a seven days a week job, each month, each year,
But he'd not begrudge a minute, of that it was clear.

His complexion was ruddy from years out in the sun,
And his hands were rough from the work that he'd done
The farm was his life, now he's no longer here
The work's carried on by the son he loved dear
He was one of the best, now my prayer must be,
Lord, look after him, as he looked after me.

Margaret Leach

Life After Star

My husband has a Springer,
Of Springers she's the best,
She out-performs and out-retrieves,
She's the best of all the rest.

She makes shooting a pleasure,
"I'm so proud of her" he said,
"If I couldn't take her with me,
I might as well be dead!"

Well this year in September
With the season drawing near,
Star is carrying her leg
A problem looms I fear!

The vet said "she's pulled a muscle,
No work for her, I'm afraid ",
My other half looked desolate,
His plans were all put paid.

"I can't go shooting without my dog,
What am I to do?"
With Star taking early retirement
We didn't have a clue.

So we asked all round fellow shooters
For a young bitch ready to go,
But with Star such a hard act to follow
It would be hard to find one, I know.

In desperation I searched the computer
To see what I could see
And at last of hours of searching
There was Rosie looking at me!

Partly trained said the advert
And just sixteen months old,
So without hesitation to Oxford
To see her and thus she was sold

Very nervous and smelly and thin
She'd not been treated well,
But with her big brown eyes and spotty legs
In love with her we fell!

Within two weeks dog and master
Had bonded 'twas plain to see,
Her confidence grew, she made friends
    with Star
And quickly won me!

After several weeks of training
She went on her first shoot,
Staff and I waited nervously
Would she get praise - or the boot!

Her master is highly delighted,
He says she improves every time,

He's like a very proud father
And she's a young girl in her prime.

So when your trusty gun dog gets older
Or injured and needs to retire,
There really are young ones just waiting
To lay their feet by your fire!

Margaret Leach

From Mother's Autograph Book

Many a ship's being lost at sea
For want of tar and rudder
And many a girl has lost her boy
Through flirting with another
14/2/1918

I'm often by my mother warned
to never take a kiss.
But if I'm given one unawares
the matter sure is plain
I mustn't think of keeping it.
But give it back again.
29/5/1914

"A wise old owl sat in an oak.
The more he saw the less he spoke;
the less he spoke the more he heard,
I wish there were more like that wise
old bird."
1930

This world is full of willing people
some willing to work
and others willing to let them.
19/1/1920

The Yankees Recipe,
How To Get Rich.
Early to bed,
early to rise,
work like the Devil
then advertise.
7/6/1935

Here's to the man that kisses his wife
and kisses his wife alone.
There's many a man that kisses another man's
wife - when he ought to be kissing his own.
(-No date-)

A little good advice,
call upon a man of business on business,
on the hours of business only,
transact your business,
And go about your business.
1/3/1930

A sure as comes your Wedding day,
a broom to you I'll send,
in sunshine use the bushy part,
in storm the over end.
(-No date-)

Can't write,
bad pen,
inspiration won't come.
Best wishes,
Amen.
26/4/1930

When the farmer packs his taters up for town,
this is the top row of his sack.
O O O O O O O O O O O O O O O O O
And this is further down
. . . .
25/31

There is so much bad in the best of us;
and so much good in the worst of us.
That it ill behoves any of us,
to find fault with the rest of us.
21/7/1915

Owen Moore went away.
Owing more than he could pay.
Owen Moore came back today
owing more.
26/3/1914

If you have a half hour to spare;
never spend it with a man who hasn't.
(-No date-)

Little birds fly high,
small bees gather Honey.
It's the men that work hard,
but their wives spend their money.
(-No date-)

My Youth is all Spent

How do I know that my youth is all spent?
My get up and go has got up and went.
But in spite of it all I am able to grin
When I recall where my get up has been.

Now having lived longer my slippers are black.
I walk to the stove and puff my way back.
The reason I know my youth is all spent
My get up and go has got up and went!

Old age is golden so I've heard it said
But sometimes I wonder when I get into bed.
With my ears in a drawer and my teeth in a cup
My eyes on a table until I wake up!

But I really don't mind when I think with a grin
Of all the grand places my get up has been!
Since I've retired from life's competition
I buzy myself with complete repetition.

Ere sleep dims my eyes, I say to myself
Is there anything else should I lay on the shelf?
But I am happy to say as I chose my door
My friends are the same, perhaps even more.

I get up each morning and dust off my wits
Pick up the newspaper and read the obits.
If my name is missing I know I'm not dead
So I eat a good breakfast and go back to bed!

When I was young my slippers were red.
I could kick up my heels right over head.
When I got older my slippers were blue
But still I could dance the whole night through!

Written by Harold Endicott of Canada,
my grandmother's brother.

Lament of a Farmer's Wife

Why don't you speak in the morning
y' miserable crotchy bloke
this can't be the way to start off the day
are y' frightened you'd choke if you spoke...

You are not worth a damn in the morning
occasional grunt or a cough
and we sit there waitin' while you eat your bacon
we might as well just wonder off...

'don't expect y' to sing in the morning
or quote from the Latin or Greek
but perhaps we'd be stirred by the odd civil word
- is it too much to ask you to speak ...

well you talk to the dog in the morning
and y' blather away to yourself
even a row with a bloody dead you
- while we sit like a mug on the shelf ...

you can talk on the phone in the morning
you always sound cheerful enough
but y' sit like a ghost when you're munching your toast
- in some deep agricultural huff ...

do all farmers say nowt in the morning
is it part of the way they're brought up
there's about as much chance of a touch of romance
- from a knackered auld cross Suffolk tup ...

can you never be bright in the morning
were you always this way as a lad
give a nod or a wink as I stand at the sink
- so the kids'll still know you're their Dad ...

we're not asking for much in the morning
when the news and the forecast are bleak
but with twenty odd years of blood sweat and tears
- SURELY T' GOD Y' CAN SPEAK!!!

Farmer John is Sixty

John William Greenslade is 60 today,
As you know, I'm his sister, so must have my say.
I hope you're all ears John, and put down your knife.
'Cos tonight, minus Michael Aspel, -'This is your life'!

Mum + Dad must have been very glad
With the farming to do and their firstborn a lad.
From baby to toddler, they tried hard to steer him,
But so fussy with food, it was doubted they'd rear him.

To persuade him to eat, their hair they would tear,
This is heresay, of course – 'cos I wasn't there!
Much to his horror when he was just five
Came the news that a sweet little sister's arrived.

To 'Tivvy' to school, first the Primary, then Grammar
Back in the days of the 'bob' and the 'tanner'.
He hated swimming, was more a land-lubber
And was good at avoiding a flying board rubber!

Teachers were different when we were small –
The slipper and cane, I bet John had them all.
School was a struggle – 'tis true but alarming,
When it came to the homework – John preferred farming.

He left school at last to go farming with Dad
At that time, electric we'd only just had,
Powered by a generator, the first light on fired it
I remember it in pieces while Bill Webber re-wired it.

At the third attempt, he passed his test
And became a 'boy racer' like all the rest!
The Y.F.C. played a big part in his life –
And through it he met his future wife.

At Proficiency classes he learnt how to do
Hedge Laying, Stock Judging and Poultry Trussing too.
Brains Trust and Public Speaking he often attended
And more often than not, was Highly Commended.

His dedication to the Y.F.C. was never in doubt
He certainly put back in more than he took out.
The pick-up could be seen Whiteheathfield – bound,
At a Bradninch cross roads in a hedge once was found!

Married to Jan 1964
Lived at Bickleigh Rectory in the flat next door.
Later in the Bungalow built at Way,
More convenient for making hay –
                    Speaking of which –

Three lovely daughters came along duly
Apples of his eye – Sally, Wendy and Julie.
He engineered the revival of the Mid Devon Show
It was hard to get it off the ground I know.

Then he channelled his energies into being a J.P.
An important job, we'd all agree.
Speeders, non-payers and such crime
He decides their punishment + if they do time!

The grandchildren, I know, are a great source of fun
His other main pastime is out with the gun.
Shooting on Exmoor and sometimes at Way
A new pond's encouraged the wild duck to stay!

And lastly – if Radio Devon you have on
You might hear, once monthly, our own 'Farmer John'.
The way things are going, before long I reckon
His fame will spread + the T.V. will beckon.

A more versatile chap you're not likely to meet
He's never let the grass grow under his feet
He's led a full life – and here's to lots more
Happy + healthy, fulfilled years in store.

A very happy birthday to John, my big 'bruv'
And every good wish from me, with love.

Margaret Leach March 15th 2000

CHAPTER TWELVE
'TWAS A PROPER JOB

I hope that after reading the previous chapters, you will realise that my life, has been full of involvement in many different farming and public organisations. In my younger ambitious days, I tried to move with the times of the modern farming, including better breeding of livestock. But our situation is that none of the immediate family would wish to continue farming here, so we have done something for our enjoyment and for the enjoyment of others. By the planting of trees in such a fashion that they resemble what is now ancient woodland, with help from the public purse for a few years, we have tried to encourage those who cannot normally enjoy the sights and signs of the countryside, to come and see how their money has been spent, and how it has added beauty to the countryside. I have been so lucky to have been born and brought up on a farm in the beautiful Exe Valley here in Devon.

As far as my achievements in public life have been, I must credit the Young Farmers movement in my early days, which gave me the grounding to take offices in several organisations. When I joined the YFC, the then club leader, Mr Herbert Twose gave me these words of advice, "Put as much in to the club as you can, and you will get a lot out", and also "Leave everything in life a little better than you found it". To date, I feel that I have got much more out than I have put in. I must add my thanks to all those family and friends that have helped me along the years, and encouraged me to write this book.

'Twas a Proper Job.